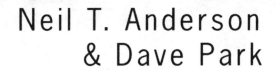

Neil T. Anderson
& Dave Park

Discover Your True
Identity in Christ and
Stop Putting Up with the
World's Garbage!

Stomping Out
the Darkness

REVISED AND UPDATED WITH STUDY GUIDE

Regal

From Gospel Light
Ventura, California, U.S.A.

Published by Regal
From Gospel Light
Ventura, California, U.S.A.
www.regalbooks.com
Printed in the U.S.A.

First Edition, 1993
Study Guide First Edition, 1995
Second Edition with Study Guide, 2007

The Library of Congress has cataloged the first edition as follows:
Anderson, Neil T., 1942-
 Stomping out the darkness / Neil T. Anderson and Dave Park.
 p. cm.
 Includes bibliographical references.
 ISBN 978-08307-4587-6 (trade paper)
 1. Identification (Religion)—Juvenile literature. 2. Junior high school students—Religious life. 3. High school students—Religious life. 4. Spiritual life—Christianity—Juvenile literature.
 I. Park, David 1961- IL Title
 BV4509.5.AS5 1993
 248.8'3-dc20

93-26385

1 2 3 4 5 6 7 8 9 10 / 11 10 09 08

Rights for publishing this book outside the U.S.A. or in non-English languages are administered by Gospel Light Worldwide, an international not-for-profit ministry. For additional information, please visit www.glww.org, email info@glww.org, or write to Gospel Light Worldwide, 1957 Eastman Avenue, Ventura, CA 93003, U.S.A.

To my wife, Grace. You are every bit of what your name implies. No one apart from Christ has ever loved me, accepted me and supported me the way you have. Thank you for seeing me in Christ.

To my kids, David Adam, Ashley Ruth and Dani Kathleen. You guys are great! Dave, thanks for crying for the lost. Ashley, thanks for requesting, "Our God Is a Handsome Guy" instead of "Our God Is an Awesome God." Dani, thanks for showing us that even a three-year-old girl can win spiritual conflicts! I love you and hope this book will help you better discover who you are in Christ!

Dave Park

CONTENTS

SMALL-GROUP STUDY GUIDE

Acknowledgments

Neil, words like "appreciate" and "thank you" just don't cut it. Your ministry has changed my life. I am so thankful to my Lord for you. You are the man God used to help me understand my true identity and bring me to freedom in Christ. Some day, Neil, when we stand before our Lord, you will see just how God has used you in my life. Then you will know how truly thankful and appreciative I am of you. Your life and example has had a great impact on me and I see Christ in you. Grace and I are grateful to you and Joanne for your sterling testimony and walk of freedom. It's so refreshing to minister with individuals who live out what God's Word teaches and truly model unconditional love and acceptance.

Thanks to Roger McNichols and the whole Freedom in Christ team for your prayers, support and guidance. You are so, so special to me. I truly love you and enjoy ministering with you.

Thanks to my special prayer partners: Larry and Joyce Beckner, Peg and Chapo McCabe, and Vera Beckner. Our intimate prayer times are dynamic and life-changing. Thanks for your transparency and love.

My thanks to Chub and Ruth Park, better known as Dad and Mom to me. Dad, you always told me I ought to write that down. Well, you said it enough times so that I finally did. Mom, thanks for your love and, of course, for your brownies. Thank you so much for the loving home you made for me and the continued support in my life.

Dave Park

FOREWORD

As a young person today, you have two absorbing concerns: First, you desperately want to gain some sense of identity; second, you want to experience the freedom to really walk with God. Few people are pointing you in the right direction, back to the pages of the Bible. Only in God's Word can you gain a sense of who you really are, and how significant and secure you are as a child of God.

I have shared many times in my speaking and writing about my own personal struggles with a poor self-image. I can say without hesitation that the realization of who I am in Christ is the single most important element in my successful walk as a Christian in ministry.

Neil and Dave have developed two much-needed books—*Stomping Out the Darkness* and *The Bondage Breaker Youth Edition*—that point you to the one place where you can gain your true identity and freedom. Your commitment to the Word of God and careful study will help you realize the power of your identity in Christ and help you become the spiritual person you want to be.

How wonderful it is to see resources specifically written for youth that address the real issues with which many young people are struggling. Standing against the spiritual forces of this fallen world and learning how to win the battle for the mind is a message that should not have any age limit.

Jesus promised us that we could live a victorious, abundant and free life. I believe those promises were made to young people as well. Neil and Dave show in a warm and insightful way how our God is in the business of stomping out the darkness and how Jesus Christ is the Bondage Breaker.

Stomping Out the Darkness and *The Bondage Breaker Youth Edition* are must-reading for every person who desires to walk free and understand the truth of who we really are in Christ.

Josh McDowell

WHO ARE YOU?

"Our hope for growth, meaning and fulfillment as Christians is based on understanding who we are as children of God."

It's the first day of the new school year. You skid into your first class just ahead of the tardy bell and grab a seat. The teacher stands and says, "I want all of you to introduce yourself to the class." Then she points a bony finger at you. "Let's begin with the latest arriver. Who are you?"

You answer confidently, "Chris Cool" (or whatever your name is).

"Wrong," she replies, "that's your name. Who are you?"

You start to sweat. "I'm the student body president."

"Wrong again, that's what you do."

"I'm an American."

"No, that's where you live."

"I'm a Baptist."

"Son, that's where you go to church."

You may also answer that you're the star quarterback on the football team or the homecoming queen or the president of the future NASA scientists club. But that's not who you are. Suppose you are seriously injured in a car accident and lose much of your physical ability or beauty or mental capacity. Would you still be you? Of course! There's much more to you than what you look like and what you do.

In 1988, Dave Dravecky, the former pitcher for the San Francisco Giants, underwent surgery for cancer on his pitching arm. The doctors thought he would never play professional baseball again. But Dave Dravecky had the heart of a lion. On August 10, 1989, he returned to the mound and won an unbelievable victory for his team.

Tragically, in his next game just five days later, his arm broke again. This time the doctors could not save it. On June 17, 1990, Dravecky checked into the hospital to have his arm and shoulder amputated.

How important was Dave Dravecky's pitching arm to him? He writes:

My arm was to me what hands are to a concert pianist, what legs are to a ballerina, what feet are to a marathon runner. It was what the people cheered me for, what they paid their hard-earned money to see. It is what made me valuable, what gave me worth, at least in the eyes of the world. Then suddenly, my arm was gone.[1]

Was Dave Dravecky's life over because he lost his arm? No! It has been radically changed, but he is still Dave Dravecky, a child of God. He realized that who he is goes far beyond his ability to throw a baseball. He continues:

When I came home from the hospital, I realized that all my son, Jonathan, wanted to do was to wrestle with me and play football on the lawn. All my daughter, Tiffany, wanted was to hug me, and all Jan, my wife, wanted was to have her husband back. They didn't care whether I had an arm or not. . . . It was enough that I was alive and that I was home.[2]

Who you are is far more than what you see on the outside. Paul, a follower of Jesus, said that we "recognize no man according to the flesh" (2 Corinthians 5:16), meaning that we shouldn't identify ourselves and others by what we look like and what we can do. But, sadly, that's what we tend to do. We want to look a certain way or achieve importance in life thinking that, when we do, we will finally be somebody.

But is who we are determined by what we do, or is what we do determined by who we are? We (Neil and Dave) go with the second statement. We believe wholeheartedly that our hope for growth, meaning and fulfillment as Christians is based on understanding who we are as children of God. If we don't know we are children of God, or if we have little idea what God's children look like and act like, we'll never act like one of them—it's impossible. Our understanding of who we are is basic to what we believe and how we behave as a Christian.

WHEN THE OUTSIDE AND INSIDE DON'T ADD UP

Several years ago a 17-year-old drove a great distance to talk with me (Neil). I have never met a girl who had so much going for her.

Mary was cover-girl pretty with a wonderful figure. She had completed 12 years of school in 11 years, graduating with a grade point average of almost 4.0. She drove a new sports car her parents gave her for graduation. I was amazed that one person could have so much.

Mary talked with me for half an hour and I realized that, though she appeared to have it all together, she was far from being together inside. She finally admitted in tears that she sometimes cried herself to sleep at night wishing she was somebody else.

Often what we show on the outside is a false front designed to disguise who we really are and cover up the secret hurts we feel about our identity. Somehow we believe that if we appear attractive or perform well or enjoy a certain amount of status, then we will have it all together on the inside as well. But that's not true. What we look like on the outside, our appearance, accomplishments and recognition, don't necessarily reflect—or produce—the peace we need inside.

We are dealing with a false equation in life. We mistakenly believe that good looks plus the popularity it brings equals a whole person. Or we feel that star performance plus great accomplishments equals a whole person. That's like trying to make one and one add up to four. It will never happen.

If these equations could work for anyone, they would have worked for Solomon. He was the king of Israel during the greatest years of its history. He had power, position, wealth, possessions and women. If a meaningful life is the result of appearance, admiration, popularity, performance, accomplishment, status or recognition, Solomon would have been the most together man who ever lived.

But God also gave the king an extra dose of wisdom to interpret his achievements. What were his comments about it all? "Meaningless! Meaningless! Utterly meaningless! Everything is meaningless!" (Ecclesiastes 1:2, NIV). We need to take a hint from a wise king: All the stuff and status we can get won't give us the personal wholeness we want and so desperately need.

We also tend to buy into the negative side of the popularity-equals-meaning equation. We believe that if a person has nothing, he or she has no hope for happiness. For example, suppose there's a guy on your campus who has a potato body and stringy hair, who stumbles when he walks and stutters when he talks. He has a bad complexion, and he fights to get Cs. Is there any hope for happiness for him?

Many kids would probably answer, "Probably not." In the earthly kingdom, where people look only at the outside, they may be right. Happiness is equated with good looks and relationships with important people. A life without these "benefits" is equated with hopelessness.

Life in God's kingdom is different. The success-equals-happiness and failure-equals-hopelessness equations don't exist. Everyone has exactly the same opportunity for a meaningful life. Why? Because, for a Christian, wholeness and meaning in life are not the products of what we have or don't have, what we've done or haven't done. If you have accepted Christ's sacrifice on the cross for your sins and believe that He rose from the dead, you are already a whole person and possess a life of infinite meaning and purpose as a child of God. The only identity equation that works in God's kingdom is you plus Christ equals wholeness and meaning.

If our identity in Christ is the key to wholeness, you may wonder, *why do so many believers have difficulty with self-worth, spiritual growth and maturity?* Because we have been deceived by the devil. Our true identity in Christ has been distorted by the great deceiver himself.

We fail, so we see ourselves as failures, which only causes us to fail more. We sin, so we see ourselves as sinners, which only causes us to sin more. We've been tricked by Satan into believing that what we do makes us what we are. This false belief sinks us deeper and deeper into the muddy pit of hopelessness and defeat. The only way out of the pit is to get a grip on who we really are as children of God.

THE GOOD THINGS WE INHERITED FROM FATHER ADAM

In order to understand who we really are, we need to understand what we inherited—good and bad—from Adam at creation. Just as we inherited physical traits from our parents and grandparents, we inherited certain traits from our first father, Adam.

Genesis 2:7 reads, "Then the Lord God formed man of dust from the ground, and breathed into his nostrils the breath of life; and man became a living being." That's where we all got our start. God created Adam, and we have all been born in his likeness.

Just like Adam, we have a physical body and an inner self (see Figure 1A). The physical body relates to the world around us through the five senses: taste, touch, smell, hearing and sight. Our inner self, sometimes called the soul, is the part of us that is created

FIGURE 1A

ORIGINAL CREATION
Genesis 1,2

PHYSICAL LIFE
United with inner self

SPIRITUAL LIFE
Inner self united with God

BODY

MIND

EMOTIONS

SPIRIT

WILL

SIGNIFICANCE:
Man had a divine purpose (Genesis 1:28).

SAFETY AND SECURITY:
All of man's needs were provided for (Genesis 1:29).

BELONGING:
Man had a sense of belonging (Genesis 2:18).

in the image of God (see Genesis 1:26-27). In our inner self we find our mind, emotions and will, allowing us to think, feel and choose. Our inner self is also spiritually connected to God.

At creation, when God breathed into Adam's nostrils the breath of life, every part of him sprang to life. Adam was fully alive both physically and spiritually. Let's talk about physical life first.

Physically Alive
We all walk around in a living, breathing earth suit made up of skin, muscle, bone, blood, fat, hair, and so forth. This is our physical body, the house that our inner self lives in. In 2 Corinthians 5:1-4, Paul refers to the believer's body as a tent, the temporary dwelling of the soul.

When we were conceived, our body was connected to our inner self. When we die, our body is separated from the inner self, and physical life ends. It's plain from this verse that the Christian's identity is more than physical attributes and skills because the body is left behind at death when our inner self goes to be with the Lord.

Even though our true identity is more than physical, in this life we can't exist without our physical body. Our inner self needs a body for physical life to be possible. And our body needs an inner self or it's no better than one of those horror-film zombies—reanimated bodies without souls.

For example, that physical brain inside your skull is like a computer, and your mind, which is part of your inner self, is like a computer programmer. A computer can't compute without a programmer, and a programmer can't program without a computer. You need your physical brain to control your movements and responses, and you need your immaterial mind to reason and make value judgments. One won't function without the other in this life.

As long as we live in the physical world, we must do so in a physical body. So we need to take care of ourselves by eating right, exercising and resting. But in reality our bodies are wasting away. They are only guaranteed for one lifetime, and then they will be thrown away. We must find our identity and significance in something more than our physical looks and abilities.

Spiritually Alive
Adam was created physically *and* spiritually alive, in perfect relationship with God. God never created mankind to live separated from or independent of God. In 2 Corinthians 4:16, Paul writes,

"Though outwardly we are wasting away, yet inwardly we are being renewed day by day" (*NIV*). He was referring to the spiritual life of the believer, which doesn't age or decay like the outer shell.

For the Christian, to be spiritually alive is for the inner self to be united with God. Like Adam, we were created to be in relationship with God. But, as we shall see later in this chapter, Adam sinned and his relationship with God, and ours as well, was broken. That's why we were born spiritually dead and why Christ came to die on the cross for us. Every person who accepts Christ's sacrifice for sin has his or her relationship with God restored (see Romans 10:13).

It is God's eternal plan to bring human creation back to Himself and restore the relationship He enjoyed with Adam at creation. That restored relationship with God, which we find only in Christ, is the basis of our identity.

Significance

Adam was extremely significant, which means he was very important. God gave him a divine purpose. He was like the king of the whole planet, ruling over all the other creatures God had created (see Genesis 1:26-27).

Satan was on the scene at creation, but he wasn't the god of this world at the time, even though he wanted that position badly. God gave that responsibility to Adam. It belonged to him until Satan tricked him out of it.

Do you know someone who is very important and significant to God? Sure you do. That significant person is *you*. Satan stole Adam's significance (and ours) when Adam sinned, but Jesus won it back for us through His death and His resurrection. That's part of our inheritance in Christ. Satan has no authority over us. Our true worth to God is now determined by Christ's death on the cross. Josh McDowell writes, "If you ever did put a price tag on yourself, it would have to read 'Jesus.' His death on the cross was the payment for our sins. You are 'worth Jesus' to God because that is what He paid for you."[3]

Safety and Security

Before Adam sinned in the garden, he enjoyed a sense of safety and security. Adam was completely cared for in the garden. He had plenty of food to eat, and there was plenty for the animals he took care of to eat (see Genesis 1:29-30). He could eat of the tree of life and live forever in God's presence. He lacked nothing.

Safety and security is another part of our inheritance in Christ. We have the riches of His kingdom at our disposal and His promise to supply all our needs (see Philippians 4:19).

Belonging

Adam and Eve experienced a sense of belonging in that perfect garden. Adam enjoyed an intimate, one-on-one relationship with God before Eve came on the scene. Then God introduced Adam to another level of belonging: "The Lord God said, 'It is not good for man to be alone; I will make him a helper suitable for him'" (Genesis 2:18). God gave Eve to Adam—and Adam to Eve—to give them a deeper sense of belonging.

The fullest sense of belonging comes from an intimate relationship with God, and that's what we have in Christ. But belonging also comes from our relationships with each other. When God created Eve, He started human companionship and community. It's not good for us to be alone. Being alone can lead to despair. God's way of preventing loneliness is to create intimacy—meaningful, open, sharing relationships with one another. In Christ we have the opportunity for intimate fellowship with God and with other believers.

BAD THINGS WE INHERITED FROM FATHER ADAM

Genesis 3 tells the sad story of Adam and Eve's fall, how they lost their relationship with God through sin when they disobeyed Him. Just as we received good things from our distant relative Adam, we also received negative side effects from his fall.

Spiritual Death

What happened to Adam and Eve spiritually because of the Fall? They died. Their relationship with God was cut off and they were separated from Him. God had specifically said, "You must not eat from the tree of the knowledge of good and evil, for when you eat of it, you will surely die" (Genesis 2:17, *NIV*). They ate and they died.

Did they die physically? No. The process of death was set in motion, but they lived on for several hundred years. Instead, they died spiritually (see Figure 1B). They lost their relationship with God. They were thrown out of the garden and banished from God's presence (see Genesis 3:23-24).

EFFECTS OF THE FALL

Genesis 3:8–4:9

REJECTED:
Therefore a need to belong!

WEAK AND HELPLESS:
Therefore a need of strength and self-control!

GUILT AND SHAME:
Therefore a need for self-worth!

Just as we inherited physical life from our first parents, we also inherited spiritual death from them (see Romans 5:12; 1 Corinthians 15:21-22; Ephesians 2:1). Every human being who comes into the world is born physically alive but spiritually dead, separated from God.

Lost Knowledge of God

What effect did the Fall have on Adam's mind? He and Eve lost their true understanding of God. We read in Genesis 3:7-8 that they tried to hide from God. Doesn't that show a broken-down understanding of who God is? How can you hide from God? After the Fall, Adam and Eve weren't thinking straight. Their mixed-up view of reality reflects Paul's description of those who don't know God: "They are darkened in their understanding and separated from the life of God because of the ignorance that is in them due to the hardening of their hearts" (Ephesians 4:18, *NIV*).

When Adam and Eve sinned, it was as if God hit the delete button on the computer in their minds. Almost everything they knew about God was gone. What they lost was not just information. Adam and Eve lost the ability to love God and experience a deep friendship and intimacy with Him.

We inherited Adam and Eve's darkened mind. Before we were saved, we knew some things *about* God, but we didn't *know* God because we had no relationship with Him. In Christ we are able to know God personally. Our relationship with God through Christ is a cornerstone of our identity.

Dominant Negative Emotions

What happened to mankind emotionally because of the Fall? For one thing, we became fearful and anxious. One of the first emotions expressed by Adam and Eve after the Fall was fear (see Genesis 3:10).

Josh McDowell tells crowds of teenagers wherever he goes, "You have two fears: the fear you'll never be loved and the fear you'll never be able to love." He's right about those fears. But have you ever asked yourself where those fears come from? We inherited them from our sinful Adam and Eve.

Two other emotional bombs that dropped on us at the Fall were shame and guilt. Before Adam and Eve sinned, they were naked and unashamed (see Genesis 2:25). God created them as sexual beings. He gave them the command to multiply, and He wasn't talking about using a calculator! Their bodies and their activities were holy.

But when they sinned, they were ashamed to be naked and they had to cover up (see Genesis 3:7). Today many people hide their inner selves in fear that others will see who they really are and reject them.

Adam and his ancestors also became depressed and angry after the Fall. Do you remember Cain, Adam and Eve's first son? He brought an offering to God and, for some reason, God was displeased with it. The Bible reports, "So Cain was very angry, and his face was downcast. Then the Lord said to Cain, 'Why are you angry? Why is your face downcast? If you do what is right, will you not be accepted?'" (Genesis 4:5-7, *NIV*).

Why was Cain angry and depressed? Because he didn't do what was right. God seemed to be saying to him, "If you just do what's right, you won't feel so bad." That's a God-given principle: If you want to feel right, you need to act right.

Too Many Choices

Adam and Eve's sin also affected their will. Do you realize that in the Garden of Eden they could only make one wrong choice? Everything they wanted to do was okay except eating from the tree of the knowledge of good and evil (see Genesis 2:16-17). Adam and Eve could make a billion good choices and only one bad choice— *only one!* That's like your parents leaving town for the weekend and telling you, "You can do anything and go anywhere you want to. Just don't drink the last can of Coke."

Eventually, however, Adam and Eve made that one bad choice. But let's not be too hard on them. We probably would have done exactly the same thing had we been in their shoes.

As a result, we are confronted every day with a ton of good and bad choices. We can choose to pray or not to pray, read our Bible or not read our Bible, go to youth group or not go to youth group. We can choose to walk according to the flesh or according to the Spirit. We face countless choices like that every day, and we eventually make some bad ones.

Attributes Become Needs

Another long-term effect of sin is that man's three glowing strengths before the Fall became three glaring needs after the Fall.

Our acceptance was replaced by rejection, so we have a need to belong. Even before the Fall, Adam had a need to belong. His need to belong to God was filled in his fellowship with God in the garden. Of all the things that were good in the garden, the only thing that was not is that Adam was alone (see Genesis 2:18). God filled that need by creating Eve.

When Adam and Eve sinned and separated themselves from God, our relationships were knocked off balance as well. We came into the world with a deep need to belong. Even when we came to Christ and filled our need to belong to God, we still need to relate to people.

That's when peer pressure is strongest. We so want to belong that sometimes we are willing to follow the bad advice of a so-called friend just to be accepted. We also fear the rejection that is heaped on us if we go against the crowd. Satan tries to use our real need for belonging to manipulate us into making poor choices about friendships and relationships.

Our innocence was replaced by guilt and shame, so we have a need for our self-worth to be restored. Many authorities agree that people today generally suffer from a poor sense of self-worth. Most secular counselors respond by telling us we're not as bad as we think and encouraging us to improve our performance. But you're not going to make people feel good about themselves by stroking their ego. Have you ever tried to tell a pretty girl with a poor self-image that she shouldn't feel that way because she's pretty? It doesn't work.

Self-worth is not an issue of giftedness, talent, intelligence or beauty. Self-worth is an identity issue. Your sense of personal worth comes from your relationship with God and knowing who you are as a child of God.

Our authority was replaced by weakness and helplessness, so we have a need for strength and self-control. You don't have to go any farther than the high school campus to see people trying to meet the need to control others and themselves. Those who are big enough just slap others around. Some buy big four-wheel-drive Toyota pickups with huge tires and drive them around school like they own the world. Still others control their world by nagging and badgering people until they get their own way.

Trying to control people and things is just an attempt to prove that we are the ruler of our own life. We may think we are in charge, but we weren't created to rule ourselves. We will either serve the true God or the god of this world, Satan.

Sinful behavior is a wrong attempt at meeting our basic needs. The real issue is: Are our needs being met by the world, the flesh and the devil, or are we allowing God to meet all our needs "according to His riches in glory in Christ Jesus" (Philippians 4:19)? It's an issue of relationship and maturity. The more we understand our identity in Christ, the more we will grow in maturity. And the more mature we become, the easier it will be for us to choose what is right.

We found out in this chapter that our true identity is not based on what we do or what we possess, but on who we are in Christ. We have reviewed the positive inheritance we received from our first parents, Adam and Eve. But we also discovered that our relationship with God and all that it entails was lost in the Fall.

There is a way out of our problem, of course. Failing Adam was followed by the super-successful Jesus Christ, whom the New Testament sometimes calls the last Adam. He won back for us the spiritual life that was lost when Adam and Eve were expelled from the garden. His triumph and what it has gained for us is the theme of the next chapter.

TRUTH ENCOUNTER

1. What did you inherit from Adam and Eve?
2. How do you think your own spiritual identity was affected by the Fall?
3. How did Christ win back the identity that we lost in the garden?
4. What do you think your friends might be basing their identity on?

Notes

1. Dave Dravecky, *When You Can't Come Back* (Grand Rapids, MI: Zondervan Publishing, 1992), p. 125.
2. Ibid., p. 126.
3. Josh McDowell, *His Image, My Image* (San Bernardino, CA: Here's Life Publishing, 1984), p. 33.

FOREVER DIFFERENT

"Many Christians . . . don't understand the dramatic change that occurred in them the moment they trusted Christ."

Imagine for a moment two typical high school guys. Let's call them Tank and Turk. These guys are into the whole high school scene. They see themselves as skin-wrapped packages of salivary glands, taste buds and sex drives. They eat anything and everything in sight, not caring about its nutritional value, and chase anything in a skirt that doesn't have hairy legs.

Tank and Turk have a special gleam in their eyes for the Barbie twins, Bobbi and Betty. Tank and Turk were chasing the sweet little Barbies around campus one day when the high school track coach noticed them. "Hey, those guys can really run!"

When the coach finally caught up with them, he said, "Why don't you guys come out for the track team?"

"Naw," they answered, watching the two Barbie twins bounce away. "We're too busy." But the coach wasn't about to take "naw" for an answer. He finally convinced the boys to at least give track a try.

So Tank and Turk started working out with the track team and discovered that they really *could* run. They began to eat properly instead of wolfing down three Big Macs apiece for lunch each day. They refused to party all night so that they could get proper rest. And soon they started winning some races.

Finally, Tank and Turk were invited to the big race at the state tournament. They arrived at the track early to stretch and warm up. Then, just minutes before the event was to start, guess who showed up: the sweet little Barbie twins, looking more beautiful and desirable then ever. They pranced up to Tank and Turk in their scanty outfits that accentuated their finest physical features. Each one was carrying a scrumptious piece of homemade Dutch apple pie with ice cream piled on top of it.

"We've missed you," they sang sweetly. "If you come with us now, you can have all this and us too."

"No way," said Tank and Turk in unison.

"Why not?" pouted the Barbies.

"Because we're runners now, and we're here to win this race."

What's different about Tank and Turk? What happened to their drives and glands? They are still the same guys who could pack away three burgers, two bags of fries and a liter of Dr. Pepper without batting an eye. And they are still the same guys who were just itching to get close to the Barbie twins. But their perception of themselves has changed. They no longer see themselves as a bundle of physical urges. Instead they see themselves as disciplined, lean, mean running machines. They came to the tournament to win a race. And the Barbie twins' offer was in conflict with why they were there and how they saw themselves.

The reason so many Christians are not enjoying the victory and freedom that is their inheritance in Christ is because they hold the wrong self-perceptions. They don't see themselves as they really are in Christ. They don't understand the dramatic change that occurred in them the moment they trusted Christ. If we don't know what God says about us and who we are in Christ, we will suffer from a poor self-image. We must get a handle on our true identity in Christ and lose our old identity in sinful Adam.

THE LIFE-CHANGING DIFFERENCE OF BEING IN CHRIST

Too many Christians identify only with Adam, whose sad story of failure is found in Genesis 1–4. We see ourselves banished from the Garden of Eden with Adam and Eve. We know we have blown it and given up paradise forever. And we can't seem to keep ourselves from repeating Adam's failure every day of our lives.

Those who have trusted Christ are no longer identified with Adam and his sin, but with Jesus and His righteousness. We are not locked outside God's presence as Adam was. We are seated with Christ in the heavenlies (see Ephesians 2:6). The difference between Adam and Christ in our personal life is eternally profound. We need to be sure we're identifying with the right one.

Unending Dependence on God

The first thing we notice about Jesus is His complete dependence on God the Father. Adam depended on God to a point. Then he became very independent, choosing to believe the serpent's lie about the tree of the knowledge of good and evil.

But Jesus was totally dependent on the Father. He said, "I can do nothing on My own initiative" (John 5:30); "I live because of the Father" (John 6:57). Also, John 8:42 and 14:10 tell us that Jesus came from the Father to do His work and to speak the words the Father wanted Him to speak.

Jesus never once depended on anything or anyone other than the Father. Even at the close of His earthly life, Jesus could say that He had done everything that God asked Him to do (see John 17:7). Jesus modeled for us what it means to live a life that is 100 percent dependent on God.

Uninterrupted Spiritual life

Another big difference between Jesus and Adam relates to spiritual life. Adam was born physically and spiritually alive; when Adam sinned, he died spiritually. After the Fall, *every* other human born on the planet has been born spiritually dead except for Jesus Christ. Like Adam, Jesus was born spiritually alive as well as physically alive.

Jesus did not keep His spiritual life a secret. He boldly proclaimed, "I am the bread of life" (John 6:48); "I am the resurrection and the life" (John 11:25); "I am the way, and the truth, and the life" (John 14:6). The apostle John got His message. He declared about Christ, "In Him was life, and the life was the light of men" (John 1:4).

But unlike Adam, Jesus did not give up His spiritual life at some point through sin. He kept His spiritual life all the way to the cross. There He died, taking the sins of the world upon Himself. He committed His spirit into His Father's hands as His physical life ended (see Luke 23:46). Then after three days, Jesus was raised from the dead. He is alive today and for all eternity. And if you have accepted Christ as your Savior, you are no longer spiritually dead but alive in Christ now and forever.

WHAT A DIFFERENCE CHRIST'S DIFFERENCE MAKES IN US!

The difference between our sinful ancestor Adam and our Savior Jesus Christ spells the difference between life and death for us. This life-giving difference is shown in 1 Corinthians 15:22: "As in Adam all die, so also in Christ all shall be made alive."

Look at the phrase "in Christ." Everything that we're going to talk about in the chapters that follow is based on the fact that believers are in Christ. Being in Christ, and all that it means to the Christian's maturity and freedom, is the overwhelming theme of the New Testament. We're *not* in Adam; we're in Christ, and being in Christ is the most important part of our identity.

New Life Requires New Birth

"But wait," you may be saying. "We weren't born in Christ. We were born in sin, thanks to Adam."

You're right! So what is God's plan for transforming us from being in Adam to being in Christ? Jesus answered that when He said to Nicodemus, "I tell you the truth, no one can see the kingdom of God unless he is born again" (John 3:3, *NIV*). Physical birth only gains us physical life. Spiritual life, the eternal life that Jesus promises to anyone who comes to Him, is only gained through spiritual birth (see John 3:30).

What does it mean to be spiritually alive in Christ? Let's compare it to physical birth. When you were born into this world, you left the dark womb and entered into a personal relationship with your parents. When you were born again, your inner self or soul left the darkness of sin and you came into a relationship with God.

When you were born physically, your parents wrote your name on a birth certificate and you became a citizen of this world. When you were born spiritually, God wrote your name in Jesus' book of life (see Revelation 21:27) and you became a citizen of heaven.

Our spiritual relationship with God is the same relationship Adam enjoyed with God before the Fall. But unlike Adam, our relationship with God is complete and eternal because it is provided by Christ. As long as Christ remains alive spiritually, we will remain alive spiritually—and that's forever.

Eternal life is not something you get when you die. If you have trusted in Christ, you are spiritually alive in Him right now. The only thing that will change when you die physically is that you will exchange your old earthbound body for a new one. But your spiritual life in Christ, which began when you personally trusted Him, will just continue on.

Salvation is not a future addition; it's a present transformation. And that change started at spiritual birth. The moment you said yes to Christ, the old sinful self you inherited from Adam was gone. Your new self in Christ is here forever. Eternal life is something you possess right now because you're in Christ

New Life Brings New Identity

Being a Christian is not just a matter of getting something; it's a matter of being someone. A Christian is not simply a person who *gets* forgiveness, who *gets* to go to heaven, who *gets* the Holy Spirit, who *gets* a new nature. A Christian, in terms of our deepest identity, is a saint, a holy one, a spiritually born child of God, a divine masterpiece, a child of light, a citizen of heaven. Being born again changed you into someone who didn't exist before. What you get from God isn't the point; it's who you are. It's not what you do as a Christian that determines who you are; it's who you are that determines what you do (see 2 Corinthians 5:17; Ephesians 2:10; 1 Peter 2:9-10; 1 John 3:1-2).

Understanding our identity in Christ is absolutely essential to our success at living the Christian life. We can't consistently behave in a way that's different from the way we see or think about ourselves. If you think you're no good, you'll probably live like you're no good. But if you see yourself as a child of God who is spiritually alive in Christ, you'll begin to live in victory and freedom as He lived. Next to a knowledge of God, a knowledge of who you are in Christ is by far the most important truth you can possess.

Are you aware that there is someone alive and active in the world today who is dead set against us seeing ourselves as spiritually alive and complete in Christ? It's Satan, of course. Satan can do nothing to damage our position and identity in Christ. But if he can deceive us into believing his lie—that we're not acceptable to God and that we'll never amount to anything as Christians—then we will live as if we have no position or identity in Christ. Satan's deception concerning our relationship with God is his major weapon against our growth and maturity in Christ.

New Life Results in a New Title

Have you noticed that one of the most frequently used words that identify Christians in the New Testament is "saint"? The word "saint" literally means "holy person." Yet Paul and other New Testament writers used "saint" to describe common, everyday Christians like us. For example, Paul's greeting in 1 Corinthians 1:2 reads, "To the church of God which is in Corinth . . . saints by calling, with all who in every place call upon the name of our Lord Jesus Christ."

Did you notice that Paul didn't say we are saints by hard work? He clearly states that we are saints by calling. Some of us have bought into the idea that a saint is someone who has earned this lofty title by living a good life or achieving a certain level of maturity. No way! The Bible says we are saints because God calls us saints.

Many Christians say, "I'm just a sinner saved by grace." But are we really sinners? No, that's what we were before we accepted Christ. God doesn't call us sinners; He calls us saints—holy ones, children of God who are spiritually alive. If you think of yourself as a sinner, guess what you will do: You'll probably live like a sinner; you'll sin. Why not identify yourself for who you really are—a saint who unfortunately happens to sin, sometimes several times a day. Remember: What you do doesn't determine who you are; who you are determines what you do.

WHAT IS TRUE OF CHRIST IS TRUE OF YOU

Since you are a saint in Christ by God's calling, you share in Christ's inheritance. What is true of Jesus now applies to you, because you are in Christ. It's part of your identity.

The paraphrased list below shows who you really are in Christ since your spiritual birth. You can't earn or buy these traits. They are guaranteed to you by the Word of God simply because you were born into God's family by faith in Christ.

Who am I?

I am the salt of the earth (Matthew 5:13).
I am the light of the world (Matthew 5:14).
I am a child of God (John 1:12).
I am part of the true vine, and Christ's life flows through me (John 15:1,5).
I am Christ's friend (John 15:15).
I am chosen by Christ to bear fruit (John 15:16).

I am Christ's personal witness sent out to tell everybody about Him (Acts 1:8).

I am a slave of righteousness (Romans 6:18).

I am a slave to God, making me holy and giving me eternal life (Romans 6:22).

I am a child of God; I can call Him my Father (Romans 8:14-15; Galatians 3:26; 4:6).

I am a coheir with Christ, inheriting His glory (Romans 8:17).

I am a temple—a dwelling place—for God. His Spirit and His life live in me (1 Corinthians 3:16; 6:19).

I am joined forever to the Lord and am one spirit with Him (1 Corinthians 6:17).

I am a part of Christ's Body (1 Corinthians 12:27).

I am a new person. My past is forgiven and everything is new (2 Corinthians 5:17).

I am at peace with God, and He has given me the work of helping others find peace with Him (2 Corinthians 5:18-19).

I am a child of God and one with others in His family (Galatians 3:26-28).

I am a child of God and will receive the inheritance He has promised (Galatians 4:6-7).

I am a saint, a holy person (Ephesians 1:1; Philippians 1:1; Colossians 1:2).

I am a citizen of heaven seated in heaven right now (Ephesians 2:6; Philippians 3:20).

I am God's building project, His handiwork, created in Christ to do His work (Ephesians 2:10).

I am a citizen of heaven with all of God's family (Ephesians 2:19).

I am a prisoner of Christ so that I can help others (Ephesians 3:1; 4:1).

I am righteous and holy (Ephesians 4:24).

I am hidden with Christ in God (Colossians 3:3).

I am an expression of the life of Christ because He is my life (Colossians 3:4).

I am chosen of God, holy and dearly loved (Colossians 3:12; 1 Thessalonians 1:4).

I am a child of light, not of darkness (1 Thessalonians 5:5).

I am chosen to share in God's heavenly calling (Hebrews 3:1).

I am part of Christ; I share in His life (Hebrews 3:14).

I am one of God's living stones, being built up in Christ as
a spiritual house (1 Peter 2:5).

I am a member of a chosen race, a royal priesthood, a holy
nation, a people belonging to God (1 Peter 2:9-10).

I am only a visitor to this world in which I temporarily live
(1 Peter 2:11).

I am an enemy of the devil (1 Peter 5:8).

I am a child of God, and I will be like Christ when He
returns (1 John 3:1-2).

I am born again in Christ, and the evil one—the devil—cannot touch me (1 John 5:18).

I am *not* the great "I am" (Exodus 3:14; John 8:24,28,58),
but by the grace of God, I am what I am (1 Corinthians
15:10).

If you are in Christ, every one of these statements is completely true of you. They won't be more true when you're a legal adult
and move out of the house. They won't be more true if you attend a
prestigious Bible college. They won't be more true if you decide to
serve in Africa as a missionary. They were true the moment you
accepted Christ, and they are true now. They are not true because
of anything you have done. They are true because of what Jesus has
done for you.

But you can make these traits about you more meaningful
and productive in your life by simply choosing to believe what
God has said about you. One of the best ways to grow into maturity in Christ is to remind yourself who you are in Christ. In our
conferences, we have the audience read the "Who Am I?" list aloud
together. We suggest that you stop right now and read the list
aloud to yourself. Come on, don't skip this part; it's really important. In fact, you should read the list at least two or three times a
day for a week or two. Memorize the verses that are especially
meaningful to you.

Read the list when you think Satan is trying to deceive you
into believing you are a worthless failure. The more you reaffirm
who you are in Christ, the more your behavior will begin to reflect
your true identity. Believing what God says about you doesn't

make it true. It is true; therefore, we believe it. It isn't prideful to believe what God says about you, but it is defeating if you don't.

THE BRIGHT HOPE OF BEING A CHILD OF GOD

As children of sinful Adam, we were helpless and hopeless. There was nothing about us to make us acceptable to God (see Romans 3:10-12,23). But God's love overruled our unloveliness. Through Jesus, God provided the only way for us to become part of His family. You are no longer a spiritual orphan; you are a child of God. As a child in God's family, you are given God's nature and His riches.

If you're beginning to think you are someone very special as a Christian, you're right. You *are* special! You're not special because you did anything for God. We don't have the ability or power to do anything for Him. It's all God's doing. All you did was respond to God's invitation to be His child. But as a child of God by being in Christ you have every right to enjoy your special relationship with your heavenly Father.

Look again at how much God loves you. First John 3:1-3 says:

See how great a love the Father has bestowed upon us, that we should be called the children of God; and such we are. . . . Beloved, now we are children of God, and it has not appeared as yet what we shall be. We know that, when He appears, we shall be like Him, because we shall see Him just as He is. And everyone who has this hope fixed on Him purifies himself, just as He is pure.

What is the believer's hope? That we are children of God *now*! And the person whose confidence is in being a child of God "purifies himself"; in other words, we begin to live like the children of God we are. We must see ourselves as children of God in order to live like children of God.

Are you a child of God? The Bible says that "as many as received Him, to them He gave the right to become children of God, even to those who believe in His name" (John 1:12). Have you received Him into your life? Do you believe Him? Would you like to receive Him? Simply express your choice by saying the following prayer:

Lord Jesus, I need You. Thank You for dying on the cross for my sins. I believe that You were resurrected from the dead in order that I might have spiritual life. I put my trust for eternal life in You and invite You into my life to be my Lord and Master. I no longer want to live independently of You. Thank You for giving me eternal life. In Jesus' name, I pray. Amen.

TRUTH ENCOUNTER

1. Why do you think it is important that you identify with the last Adam, Jesus? What effect does that have on you?
2. What does your new life in Christ bring to you?
3. How do you think God feels about you now that you are in Christ?
4. What do you think might keep you from walking in Christ?

Note
1. David C. Needham, *Birthright/ Christian Do You Know Who You Are?* (Portland, OR: Multnomah Press, 1981), adapted from an illustration on p. 73.

SEE YOURSELF FOR WHO YOU REALLY ARE

"Your perception of your identity makes a big difference in your success at dealing with the challenges and conflicts in your life."

Claire attended a church college ministry I (Neil) was involved in several years ago. On an earthly level, Claire had absolutely nothing going for her. She had a dumpy figure and a bad complexion. Her father was a drunken bum who had deserted the family. Her mother worked two jobs just to make ends meet. Her older brother, a drug addict, was always in and out of the house.

Was there any way she could compete for acceptance in a world that seems only to be attracted to physical beauty and material success? I didn't think so. But to my surprise, everyone in the college group liked Claire and loved to be around her. She had lots of friends. And eventually she married the nicest guy in our college department.

What was Claire's secret? Claire accepted herself for who God said she was in Christ: a child of God. And she confidently committed herself to God's main goal for her life: to be like Christ and to love people. She was so positive and caring toward others that everyone loved her.

BELIEF BEFORE BEHAVIOR

Claire's experience reminds us how important it is to base our Christian lives on what we believe instead of how we behave. We need a firm grip on what God says about who we are before we will experience much success at living the Christian life. A healthy Christian lifestyle is the result of a healthy Christian belief system, not the other way around.

For example, the Bible tells us to "stand firm against the schemes of the devil" (Ephesians 6:11). But how can we hope to stand firm against the devil if we don't understand that God has already raised us up with Christ and seated us victoriously with Him in heavenly places (see Ephesians 2:6)? How can we rejoice and be strong during trials (see Romans 12:12) without the confidence of knowing we have been made right with God by faith and enjoy peace with Him through Christ (see Romans 5:1)?

If what we believe about God and ourselves is shaky, then our day-to-day behavior will be shaky. But when our belief system and our relationship with God are based on what He says is true, we'll have very little trouble working out the practical aspects of daily Christianity.

Get a Grip on God's Grace

The importance of believing what God says about us in spite of difficult experiences was brought home to me (Dave) through the life of a very special young girl named Myndee Hudson. Myndee was a junior high girl with long, beautiful blonde hair. I met her while speaking at a camp in Montana. She was unable to attend some of my talks and later apologized for her absence, saying she was sick.

As it turned out, Myndee was more than sick. Just two days after camp, Myndee was rushed to Denver, Colorado, for delicate emergency surgery to remove a malignant tumor invading her brain stem and spinal cord. The surgery lasted 12 hours. During recovery she developed pneumonia. Myndee's condition was so serious that doctors offered her family little hope that she would live out the rest of that year.

But Myndee was a believer and a fighter. She found a portion of Scripture to guide her through her battles. Romans 8:35-38 seemed to be written just for her:

> Who shall separate us from the love of Christ? Shall trouble or hardship or persecution or famine or nakedness or danger or sword? . . . No, in all these things we are more than conquerors through him who loved us. For I am convinced that neither death nor life, neither angels nor demons, neither the present nor the future, nor any powers, neither height nor depth, nor anything else in all creation,

will be able to separate us from the love of God that is in Christ Jesus our Lord (*NIV*).

Myndee held on to these words because they were more than words to her. They were *truth*. She recovered from surgery and pneumonia and started chemotherapy. The radiation treatments made her sick and she lost most of her hair.

When I visited Myndee in her home, she met me at the door wearing a blonde wig. She had lost over 20 pounds. Her voice was raspy from the radiation treatments, and she looked very weak.

"How are you doing, Myndee?" I asked, fighting back my tears.

Myndee broke the pain of the awkward moment with a smile, saying, "Do you want to see my wig?" Before I could respond she pulled the wig off her head and thrust it toward me. Her beautiful, long blonde hair was gone except for small patches draped from her head like thin strands of ribbon.

This was no vain girl who was devastated at the loss of her physical beauty. This was a girl who had found a new and greater beauty inside because of her relationship with God in Christ.

"Dave, I wish every kid could have cancer," Myndee said as we talked.

I couldn't hide my look of shock. "Myndee, why?"

She smiled her cute little smile and said, "Because then they would realize what's really important in life. The only things my friends seem to care about are things that don't last: boyfriends, what your hair looks like, who likes you. It's all so unimportant compared to knowing God. I used to be that way too." She paused for a moment and then smiled at me. "But when you know you're going to die, you only care about things that are going to last. Before I was sick, Jesus was only a part of my life. Now He's everything to me."

Myndee Hudson died before she got out of junior high school. But she learned more and affected more lives for Christ than many Christians who live decades longer. Her message to us is: "Seek first His kingdom and His righteousness" (Matthew 6:33). Nothing else is very important compared to getting right with God and knowing who you are in Christ.

Getting right with God always begins with settling once and for all the issue that God is your loving Father and you are His accepted child. That's the basic truth of your spiritual identity. You are a child of God, you are created in His image, you have been declared righteous by Him because you have put your trust in Christ.

As long as we believe that and walk accordingly, our daily experience of walking with Christ will result in growth. But when we get our eyes off our identity and try instead to become something we aren't, or wish we were somebody else, we'll struggle. We need to learn as Myndee learned that we don't serve God to gain His acceptance; we are accepted, so we serve God. We don't follow Him in order to be loved; we are loved, so we follow Him.

That's why we are called to live by faith (see Romans 1:16-17). The key to the victorious Christian life is believing who God is, believing who we are in Christ and believing what God says about our relationship with Him.

Do we have a choice? Of course! Satan will try to convince us that we are unworthy, unacceptable, sin-sick people who will never amount to anything in God's eyes. Is that true? Absolutely not! We are saints whom God has declared righteous. Believing Satan's lie will result in a defeated, fruitless life. But believing God's truth about our identity will set us free.

The Fallout from God's Grace

The paraphrased list below further describes your identity in Christ. Read this list aloud to yourself repeatedly until it becomes a part of you. Pray through the list occasionally, asking God to cement these truths in your heart:

Since I am in Christ, by the grace of God . . .

I am now acceptable to God (justified) and completely forgiven. I live at peace with Him (Romans 5:1).
The sinful person I used to be died with Christ, and sin no longer rules my life (Romans 6:1-6).
I am free from the punishment (condemnation) my sin deserves (Romans 8:1).
I have been placed into Christ by God's doing (1 Corinthians 1:30).
I have received God's Spirit into my life. I can recognize the blessings He has given me (1 Corinthians 2:12).
I have been given the mind of Christ. He gives me His wisdom to make right choices (1 Corinthians 2:16).

I have been bought with a price; I am not my own; I belong to God (1 Corinthians 6:19-20).

I am God's possession, chosen and secure in Him (sealed). I have been given the Holy Spirit as a promise of my inheritance to come (2 Corinthians 1:21-22; Ephesians 1:13-14).

Since I have died, I no longer live for myself, but for Christ (2 Corinthians 5:14-15).

I have been made acceptable to God (righteous) (2 Corinthians 5:21).

I have been crucified with Christ and it is no longer I who live, but Christ lives in me. The life I now live is Christ's life (Galatians 2:20).

I have been blessed with every spiritual blessing (Ephesians 1:3).

I was chosen in Christ to be holy before the world was created. I am without blame before Him (Ephesians 1:4).

I was chosen by God (predestined) to be adopted as His child (Ephesians 1:5).

I have been bought out of slavery to sin (redeemed) and forgiven. I have received His generous grace (Ephesians 1:7-8).

I have been made spiritually alive just as Christ is alive (Ephesians 2:5).

I have been raised up and seated with Christ in heaven (Ephesians 2:6).

I have direct access to God through the Spirit (Ephesians 2:18).

I may approach God with boldness, freedom and confidence (Ephesians 3:12).

I have been rescued from the dark power of Satan's rule and have been brought into the kingdom of Christ (Colossians 1:13).

I have been forgiven of all my sins and set free. The debt against me has been cancelled (Colossians 1:14).

Christ Himself lives in me (Colossians 1:27).

I am firmly rooted in Christ and am now being built up in Him (Colossians 2:7).

I am fully grown (complete) in Christ (Colossians 2:10).

I am spiritually clean. My old sinful self has been removed (Colossians 2:11).

I have been buried, raised and made alive with Christ (Colossians 2:12-13).

I died with Christ and I have been raised up with Christ. My life is now hidden with Christ in God. Christ is now my life (Colossians 3:1-4).

I have been given a spirit of power, love and self-control (2 Timothy 1:7).

I have been saved and set apart (sanctified) according to God's plan (2 Timothy 1:9; Titus 3:5).

Because I am set apart (sanctified) and one with Christ, He is not ashamed to call me His brother or sister (Hebrews 2:11).

I have the right to come boldly before the throne of God. He will meet my needs lovingly and kindly (Hebrews 4:16).

I have been given great and valuable promises. God's nature has become a part of me (2 Peter 1:4).

Kristy, a high schooler, attended a Bible study at my (Dave's) home. We were studying one of Neil Anderson's other books, *The Bondage Breaker*. After the Bible study, Kristy asked if she could talk with me. It was a warm night, so we stepped outside and left the crowd in the living room.

Gazing up at the sky, Kristy's eyes filled with tears. "I don't think anybody loves me," she said. Her words reflected her continuing struggle with her family, an eating disorder and an all-around poor self-image.

"Kristy, do you remember the two lists I shared during the study recently, 'Who Am I' and 'Since I Am in Christ'?"

"Yes," she said softly.

"Do you believe that those statements are true of you?"

"Oh, I don't know," she said. The frustration in her voice was obvious.

"Let me read them to you again. Better yet, why don't you read them to me?"

She agreed and began to read the statements. At first her tone lacked enthusiasm. But gradually a change occurred. Her voice became more confident and a smile began to appear. By the time she finished the lists, she was even laughing.

Isn't that incredible? Did any of Kristy's circumstances change as she read the statements? No, nothing changed except her understanding of who she is in Christ.

Your perception of your identity makes a big difference in your success at dealing with the challenges and conflicts of your life. It is very important to your growth and maturity that you believe God's truth about who you are.

THERE'S A DIFFERENCE BETWEEN RELATIONSHIP AND FELLOWSHIP

With all this emphasis on God's complete acceptance of us in Christ, you may be wondering, *what happens to our relationship with God when we sin? Doesn't our sin block God's acceptance of us?* No, as the following story illustrates.

When I (Neil) was born physically, I had a father. His name was Marvin Anderson. As his son, I not only have Marvin Ander-son's last name, but I have Marvin Anderson's blood flowing through my veins. Marvin Anderson and Neil Anderson are blood-related.

Is there anything that I could possibly do that would change my blood relationship to my father? What if I ran away from home and changed my name? What if he kicked me out of the house? What if he disowned me? Would I still be his son? Of course! We're related by blood and nothing can change that.

But is there anything I could do that would affect how we get along as father and son? Yes, indeed—and by the time I was five years old I had discovered almost every way! My relationship with my father was never in jeopardy, but the harmony of our relationship was interrupted countless times by my behavior.

What was the key issue to harmony with my father? Obedience. The relationship issue was settled for life when I was born into Dad's family as his son. The harmony issue was addressed repeatedly as a result of my behavior and misbehavior. I discovered very early in life that if I obeyed Dad, I lived in harmony with him. If I didn't obey him, we were out of harmony. But whether we were in harmony or not, he was always my father.

In the spiritual realm, when I was born again I became a member of God's family. God is my Father and I enjoy an eternal relationship with Him through the precious blood of Christ (see

1 Peter 1:18-19). As a son of God, is there anything I can do that will change my relationship with Him? No! I'm related to God by spiritual birth and nothing can change that blood relationship. As Myndee Hudson discovered in Romans 8:35, nothing can separate us from the love of Christ. Jesus declared, "My sheep hear My voice . . . and I give eternal life to them, and they shall never perish; and no one shall snatch them out of My hand" (John 10:27-28). My relationship with God was forever settled when I was born into His family.

But is there anything I can do that will interfere with the harmony of my relationship with God? Absolutely. Harmony with God is based on the same issue as harmony with my earthly father: obedience. When I obey God, I live in harmony with Him. When I don't obey God, the harmony of our relationship is disturbed and my life is usually miserable as a result.

I love my heavenly Father and I want to be in harmony with Him, so I try to obey Him. But even when we are not in harmony because of my disobedience, my relationship with Him is not at stake because we are related by the blood of Jesus Christ.

So where should you place your effort in the process of spiritual growth and maturity? Not on your relationship to God, because there's nothing you can do to improve upon it other than continuing to believe that it is true. You are a child of God—period. You can't become any more of a child of God than what your spiritual birth made you. The harmony of your relationship with God that is determined by your diligent efforts to obey Him will result in spiritual maturity.

BELIEVE WHAT YOU PERCEIVE IN OTHERS

Tony Campolo tells a great story about a boy named Teddy Stallard. Teddy was an unattractive, unmotivated child whose mother died when he was in the third grade. Nobody liked Teddy, including his fifth-grade teacher, Miss Thompson.

It was Christmastime of Teddy's fifth grade and the children in Miss Thompson's class brought her Christmas presents. They piled their presents on her desk and crowded around to watch her open them. Among the presents was one from Teddy. She was surprised that he had brought her a gift. Teddy's gift was wrapped in brown paper and was held together with scotch tape. On the paper were written the simple words, "For Miss Thompson from Teddy." When she opened Teddy's present, out fell a gaudy rhinestone bracelet, with half the stones missing, and a bottle of cheap perfume.

The other boys and girls began to giggle and smirk over Teddy's gifts, but Miss Thompson at least had enough sense to silence them by immediately putting on the bracelet and putting some of the perfume on her wrist. Holding her wrist up for the other children to smell, she said, "Doesn't that smell lovely?" And the children, taking their cue from the teacher, readily agreed with "oohs" and "ahhs."

At the end of the day when school was over and the other children had left, Teddy had lingered behind. Slowly he came over to her desk and said softly, "Miss Thompson . . . Miss Thompson, you smell like my mother and her bracelet looks real pretty on you, too. I'm glad you like my presents." When Teddy left, Miss Thompson got down on her knees and asked God to forgive her.

The next day when the children came to school, they were welcomed by a new teacher. Miss Thompson had become a different person. She was no longer just a teacher; she had become an agent of God. She helped all the children, especially the slow ones and especially Teddy Stallard. Teddy showed dramatic improvement. He had caught up with most of the students and was even ahead of some.

She didn't hear from Teddy for a long time. Then one day, she received a note that read:

Dear Miss Thompson:
    I want you to be the first to know. I will be graduating second in my class.
    Love,
    Teddy Stallard

Four years later, another note came:

Dear Miss Thompson:
    They just told me I will be graduating first in my class. I wanted you to be the first to know. The university has not been easy, but I like it.
    Love,
    Teddy Stallard

And four years later:

Dear Miss Thompson:
    As of today I am Theodore Stallard, M.D.
How about that?
    I wanted you to be the first to know. I
am getting married next month, the 27th to
be exact. I want you to come sit where my
mother would sit if she were alive. You are
the only family I have now; Dad died last
year.
    Love,
    Teddy Stallard

Miss Thompson went to that wedding and sat where Teddy's mother would have sat. She deserved to sit there; she had done something for Teddy that he could never forget.[1]

As important as it is for you to believe in your true identity as a child of God, it is equally important that you see other Christians for who they are and treat them the way they should be treated. We often treat people the way we see them. If we believe they are losers, we treat them like losers, and so many of them act like losers. But if we see our brothers and sisters in Christ as children of God, we will treat them as children of God and they will find it easier to live like children of God.

The New Testament clearly states that we are saints who sin (see 1 John 1:8). But we are not to focus on one another's sins. Instead, we are called to *accept* each other and build each other up. In fact, if we could memorize just one verse from the New Testament, put it into practice and never violate it, we would probably resolve many of the problems in our homes and churches. The verse is Ephesians 4:29: "Let no unwholesome word proceed from your mouth, but only such a word as is good for edification according to the need of the moment, that it may give grace to those who hear."

Isn't it amazing that you and I have the power to give grace to others through the proper use of our words? If we said nothing to put others down, and only built up others as Ephesians 4:29 commands, we would be part of God's construction crew instead of members of Satan's wrecking crew.

BELiEViNG THE TRUTH ABOUT YOURSELF

One of the most dramatic turnarounds I (Neil) have witnessed in someone occurred in Jenny. Twenty-three-year-old Jenny was a pretty Christian girl with a seemingly pleasant personality. She had loving parents and came from a good church. But she was torn up inside and deeply depressed. She had bombed out of college and was on the verge of being fired from her job. She had suffered from eating disorders for several years without relief.

Jenny claimed to be a Christian, so I challenged her with the biblical truth of who she was in Christ. I kept sharing with her the good news of her spiritual identity. Finally she said, "Are you always this positive?"

"It's not a matter of being positive, Jenny," I answered. "It's a matter of believing the truth. Because of your relationship with God, this is who you are in Christ." She left our meeting with a glimmer of hope. Several weeks later Jenny attended a one-month spiritual retreat at my invitation. Shortly after we arrived, I sat down with Jenny privately. "I didn't invite you here to change your behavior, Jenny," I said. "Your behavior isn't your problem."

"I've always been told that my behavior is my problem," she answered, looking a little surprised at my statement. "Everyone I know is trying to change my behavior."

"I'm not worried about your behavior. It's your beliefs I'm interested in. I want to change your beliefs about who God is and who you are in Christ. You're not a failure. You're not a sick individual who is a problem to your parents and to your church. You are a child of God, no better and no worse than any other person at this retreat. I want you to start believing it, because it's the truth."

For the first time in her life Jenny had been affirmed as the person of value to God that she was. And she began to believe it. During the next 30 days, a miraculous transformation took place in Jenny. The changes were nothing less than dramatic.

What changed in Jenny? Her beliefs about God and herself. She was a child of God by faith all along. She just began to walk by faith, seeing herself for who she really is in Christ. Her behavior began to conform to the truth about her spiritual identity. Will Jenny's behavior continue to improve? Yes, as long as she continues to believe God and live in harmony with Him by obeying His commandments.

You are a righteous, accepted child of God. No matter what else you have been taught or believe about yourself, your identity in Christ is solid Bible truth. Read and reread the identity statements listed in this chapter and the last. See yourself in them. Believe them. Walk in them. And your behavior as a Christian will conform to what you believe as you walk by faith.

TRUTH ENCOUNTER

1. What did you learn from Claire's and Myndee's stories?
2. What is the difference between your relationship with God and living in harmony with Him?
3. How should you perceive other believers? Who do you need to "accept" and how can you do it?
4. Why is what you believe more important than how you behave? What Scripture verses and truths about yourself do you need to memorize?

Note

1. Anthony Campolo, *Who Switched the Price Tags?* (Dallas, TX: Word, 1987), adapted from pp. 67-72.

SOMETHING OLD, SOMETHING NEW

"When you came into spiritual relationship with God through your new birth, you didn't add a new, divine nature to your old, sinful nature. You exchanged natures."

Our spiritual identity is anchored to the truth that we are saints who sin, not sinners. Because of God's grace and our faith in Christ, we have been born again. We are spiritually alive and we enjoy a relationship with God as Adam and Eve did before the Fall. Being in Christ, we are forgiven, justified and completely acceptable to God. Understanding and acting upon this truth of who we are in Christ is the basis for our growth and victory.

But we have also discovered that, despite God's provision for us in Christ, we are still far from perfect in our behavior. We are saints who sin. Our position in Christ is settled and solid. But our daily actions are often marked by failure and disobedience, which disturb the harmony of our relationship with God. This is our biggest problem as Christians. We groan with the apostle Paul: "When I want to do good, I don't. And when I try not to do wrong, I do it anyway. Oh, what a miserable person I am!" (Romans 7:19,24, *NLT*).

When we talk about the problems of disobedience that make us feel more like sinners than saints, a lot of interesting terms pop up: old nature, old self (or old man), flesh and sin. What do these terms really mean? Are we saints or not? And if we are, why do we sometimes live like we're not?

These are tough questions for Christians of any age. Bible scholars have wrestled with them for centuries, and we don't pretend to have the final answers in this book. But in this chapter we want to talk about some of the terms that often confuse Christians who are trying to deal with the sinful side of their sainthood.

The more we understand about our old sinful self, our new self in Christ and the sin that bothers us, angers us and embarrasses us, the better prepared we will be to grow in our identity in Christ.

FROM SINNER TO SAINT

Colossians 1:13 says that God "delivered us from the domain of darkness, and transferred us to the kingdom of His beloved Son." We have changed kingdoms—from Satan's to God's; we are not members of both.

God declares that we "are not in the flesh but in the Spirit" (Romans 8:9). We're one or the other, not half and half. Ephesians 5:8 states that "you were formerly darkness, but now you are light in the Lord." Darkness and light are not fighting for control within us. When we trusted Christ, the darkness departed and we are now light.

The Bible says, "If any man is in Christ, he is a new creature; the old things passed away; behold, the new things have come" (2 Corinthians 5:17). Does that sound like we are partly new creature and partly old creature and that the two creatures are battling for supremacy within us? Not at all.

A good illustration of what has happened to us is found in the character Eustace in C. S. Lewis's book *Voyage of the Dawn Treader* in the Narnia series. Eustace was a boy who was so awful and nasty that he turned into an ugly, evil dragon. Then he met the lion, Aslan, who represents Christ. And Aslan changed him from a dragon into a fine young man.

At first Eustace tried to change himself by scratching and peeling off layers of his dragon skin. But for every layer that came off, another layer of wrinkled, scaly skin appeared underneath. Finally Aslan stepped up to do the job. With one painful swipe of his powerful claws, the lion cut to the heart of Eustace's dragon flesh and peeled it away, and Eustace the boy stepped out

One moment Eustace was a dragon; the next moment he was a boy. He went from one to the other; he wasn't part dragon and part boy. Eustace pictures what the Bible says about us. Once we were in the kingdom of Satan; now we're in the kingdom of God. Once we were of the flesh; now we're of the Spirit. Once we were darkness; now we are light. Once we were old, sinful creatures; now we are new, saintly creatures.

If we believe that we are part light and part darkness, part saint and part sinner, we will live unfruitful lives with little to distinguish us from non-Christians. We may confess our tendency to sin and strive to do better. But we will live continually defeated lives because we think of ourselves only as sinners saved by grace who are hanging on until the rapture.

Satan knows he can do nothing about who we really are. But if he can get us to believe we are no different from non-Christians, then we will behave no differently from them.

God's work in changing sinners to saints through Christ's death and resurrection is His greatest accomplishment on Earth. Your inner change (justification), when God took away your sin and gave you His righteousness, happened the moment you trusted Christ as your Savior. That's when the dragon skin was cut away and you became a new creature. The outer change (sanctification), learning to think and act like a new creature in Christ, continues throughout life. But learning to live successfully like a new creature will only happen when you accept the truth that you already are a new creature.

The Nature of the Matter

What does the Bible specifically say about our nature? Ephesians 2:1-3 describes the nature we all shared before we came to Christ:

> And you were dead in your trespasses and sins, in which you formerly walked according to the course of this world, according to the prince of the power of the air, of the spirit that is now working in the sons of disobedience. Among them we too all formerly lived in the lusts of our flesh, indulging the desires of the flesh and of the mind, and were by nature children of wrath, even as the rest.

What was our basic nature before we were born again spiritually? We "were by nature children of wrath," dead in sin, subject to Satan's power, living completely to fulfill sinful lusts and desires. This is the condition of every unbeliever today.

Second Peter 1:3-4 describes our nature after we came to Christ:

> His divine power has granted to us everything pertaining to life and godliness, through the true knowledge of Him

who called us by His own glory and excellence. For by these He has granted to us His precious and magnificent promises, in order that by them you might become partakers of the divine nature, having escaped the corruption that is in the world by lust.

When you came into spiritual relationship with God through your new birth, you didn't *add* a new, divine nature to your old, sinful nature. You *exchanged* natures. Salvation isn't just a matter of God forgiving your sins and issuing you a ticket to heaven when you die. Salvation is a complete change. God changed you from darkness to light, from sinner to saint There is a newness about you that wasn't there before.

If God hadn't changed our identity at salvation, we would be stuck with our old identity until we died. How could we expect to grow to maturity if we didn't start as transformed children of God? Receiving God's nature is basic to our identity and maturity in Christ.

Either One or the Other

Ephesians 5:8 describes the needed change that occurs at salvation: "You were formerly darkness, but now you are light in the Lord; walk as children of light." It doesn't say we were *in* darkness; it says we *were* darkness. Darkness was our nature as unbelievers. Nor does it say we are now *in* the light; it says we *are* light. God changed our basic nature from darkness to light.

The issue in this passage is not improving our nature. Our new nature is already settled. The issue is learning how to walk in harmony with our new nature. How do we do that? By learning to walk by faith and walk in the Spirit, which are the subjects of the chapters ahead.

Why do you need the nature of Christ within you? So you can *be* like Christ, not just *act* like Him. God has not given us the power to imitate Him. He has made us partakers of His nature so that we can actually *be* like Him. We don't become Christians by acting like Christians. We are not on a performance basis with God. He doesn't say, "Here are My standards, now you measure up." He knows we can't solve the problem of an old sinful self by simply improving our behavior. He must change our nature, who we are, and give us an entirely new self—the life of Christ in us—which is the grace we need to measure up to His standards.

IS THE "OLD MAN" ALIVE, DYING OR ALREADY DEAD?

Before we came to Christ, we were sinners because it was our nature to sin. That nature was our old self. The *King James Version* often refers to our old self as our "old man." First Corinthians 2:14 in the *New American Standard Bible* calls him the "natural man" who cannot accept or understand the things of the Spirit.

Rest in Peace

What happened to the old you at salvation? You died—not the physical you, of course, but that old inner self that was powered by the old nature you inherited from Adam (see Romans 6:2-6; Colossians 3:3). What was the method of death? Crucifixion with Christ. Romans 6:6 states, "Our old self was crucified with Him, that our body of sin might be done away with, that we should no longer be slaves to sin." Paul announced in Galatians 2:20, "I have been crucified with Christ." At salvation you were placed into Christ, the One who died on the cross for your sin. Being in Christ, your old self died with Him there.

Why did the old self need to die? Romans 6:6 tells us that the old self was independent and disobedient to God, so it had to die in order that "we should no longer be slaves to sin." When your old self died with Christ on the cross, your relationship with sin ended. Your old self—the sinner—and your old nature—sinfulness—are gone forever.

Does this mean that we are now sinless? No way! The death of our old self ended our relationship with sin. But sin and Satan are still around, and they are strong and appealing. But because of the crucifixion of the old self, sin's power over us is broken (see Romans 6:7,12,14). We are no longer under any obligation to serve sin, to obey sin or to respond to sin.

We commit sin when we make a willful decision to allow ourselves to act independently of God, which is how our old self acted all the time. When we make that wrong decision, we violate our new nature and our new identity. Such actions must be confessed and turned away from.

Once Dead, Always Dead

A pastor visited me (Neil) a few years ago, and he was in real turmoil. "I've been struggling to live a victorious Christian life for 20 years. I think I know what my problem is. Colossians 3:3 says, 'For you have died and your life is hidden with Christ in God.' I've been struggling all these years because I haven't died like this verse says. How do I die, Neil?"

"Dying is not your problem," I said. "Read the verse again, just a little slower."

"'For you have died and your life is hidden with Christ in God.' I know, Neil. That's my problem. I haven't died."

"Read it once again," I pressed, "just a little bit slower."

"'For you have died—'" and suddenly a light switched on in his understanding. "Hey, that's past tense, isn't it?"

"Absolutely. Your problem isn't dying; you're already dead. You died at salvation. No wonder you've been struggling as a Christian. You've been trying to do something that's already been done, and that's impossible. The death Paul talks about in Colossians 3:3 isn't something God expects you to *do*; it's something He expects you to *know*, accept and believe. You can't do anything to become what you already are."

Christ paid the debt for our sin through His death on the cross. Thanks to Him, your old self has been replaced by a new self, controlled by a new nature, which was not there before (see 2 Corinthians 5:17). Your old self was destroyed in the death of Christ and your new self sprang to life in the resurrection of Christ (see 1 Corinthians 15:20-22). The new life that characterizes your new self is nothing less than the life of Jesus Christ implanted in you (see Galatians 2:20; Colossians 3:4).

WHERE DOES THE FLESH FIT INTO THE PICTURE?

When I (Neil) was in the Navy, we called the captain of our ship "the Old Man." Our Old Man was tough and crusty, and nobody liked him. He was not a good example of a naval officer. So when our Old Man got transferred to another ship, we all rejoiced.

Then we got a new skipper—a new Old Man. The Old Man no longer had any authority over us and we no longer had any relationship with him. But I was trained under that Old Man. So how do you think I related to the new Old Man? At first I tiptoed around him expecting him to bite my head off. That's how I had lived for two years around my first skipper.

But as I got to know the new skipper, I realized that he wasn't a crusty old tyrant like my Old Man. He was a good guy, really concerned about us. But I had been programmed for two years to react a certain way when I saw a captain's uniform. I didn't need to react that way any longer, but it took several months to recondition myself to the new skipper.

Reacting to Your Old Skipper

We once served under a cruel, self-serving skipper within us: our old sinful self with its sinful nature. The admiral of that fleet is Satan himself, the prince of darkness. But by God's grace we now have a new admiral, Jesus, and a new skipper: our new self, which is powered by the divine nature of Jesus Christ. As children of God, saints, we are no longer under the control of our Old Man. He is dead, buried, gone forever.

So why do we live as if our old skipper is still in control? Because everything we learned before we became Christians was programmed into our brains. Much of what the Bible calls "the flesh" are those programmed habits and patterns of thinking we learned from the world. The flesh is that tendency within each person to operate independently of God and to center our interests on ourselves. Unsaved people live out their lives totally in the flesh (see Romans 8:7-8; 2 Corinthians 5:15).

Since we were born physically alive but spiritually dead, we learned to live our lives independently of God, doing our own thing. During the years we spent separated from God, our worldly experiences thoroughly programmed us with thought patterns and habits that are alien to God. When we were born again, our old self died and our new self came to life. But our flesh remained. So even though our old skipper is gone, our flesh remains in opposition to God as a programmed tendency for sin— living independently of God.

Responding to Your New Skipper

There is a difference in Scripture between being in the flesh and walking according to the flesh. As a Christian, you are no longer in the flesh. That phrase describes people who are still spiritually dead (see Romans 8:8), those who live independently of God.

You are not in the flesh; you are in Christ (see Romans 8:9). You no longer live independently of God; you have declared your dependence on Him by placing faith in Christ. But even though you are not in the flesh, you may still choose to walk *according* to the flesh (see Romans 8:12-13). You may still act *according* to the flesh (see Romans 8:12-13). You may still act independently of God by saying yes to the patterns and habits programmed into your mind by the world you lived in.

Unbelievers can't help but live according to the flesh because they are totally in the flesh. But your old skipper is gone. You are no longer in the flesh and you no longer need to live according to its desires.

Getting rid of the old self was God's job, but keeping the flesh and its deeds from dominating our lives is our responsibility (see Romans 8:12). God has changed our nature, but it's our job to change our behavior by "putting to death the deeds of the body" (Romans 8:13). How do we do that? There are two major parts to gaining victory over the flesh.

First, we must learn to base our behavior on our new master and our new self, which is joined with the nature of Christ. Paul promised, "Walk by the Spirit, and you will not carry out the desire of the flesh" (Galatians 5:16). We will talk about walking in the Spirit in chapter 5. Second, our old pattern for thinking and responding to our sin-trained flesh must be transformed by the renewing of our minds (see Romans 12:2). Renewing the mind is the topic of chapters 6 to 9.

WHAT ROLE DOES SIN PLAY IN OUR STRUGGLE TOWARD SAINTLY BEHAVIOR?

When you received Christ, the power of sin was not broken, but its power to dominate *you* was broken through your death, resurrection and righteousness in Christ (see Romans 6:7; 8:10). You no longer have to sin because you are dead to sin and alive to God in Christ (see Romans 6:11). Sin still strongly appeals to your flesh to continue to act independently of God. But you no longer have to sin like you did before receiving Christ. It is your responsibility not to let sin reign in your life (see Romans 6:12). You do that by not allowing your thoughts, eyes, hands, feet and such to be used for sinful purposes (see Romans 6:13).

Doing What I Don't Want to Do
Perhaps the best description of a believer's struggle with sin is found in Romans 7:15-25. In verses 15 and 16, Paul describes the

problem: "I do not understand what I do. For what I want to do I do not do, but what I hate I do. And if I do what I do not want to do, I agree that the law is good" (*NIV*).

Notice that there is only one player in these two verses—the "I," mentioned nine times. Also notice that this person has a good heart; he agrees with the law of God. But this good-hearted Christian has a behavior problem. He knows what he should be doing but, for some reason, he can't do it. He agrees with God but ends up doing the very things he hates. Does that sound like every Christian young person you know?

Verse 20 uncovers the reason for this behavior problem: "If I do what I do not want to do, it is no longer I who do it, but it is sin living in me that does it" (*NIV*). How many players are involved now? Two: "sin" and "me." Sin dwelling in me prevents me from doing what I want to do. Whenever that happens, I am responsible for allowing sin to reign and for getting rid of it.

Do these verses say that I am no good, that I am evil or that I am sin? Absolutely not. They say that I have something dwelling in me that is evil and sinful, but it's not me. If I have a sliver in my finger, I could say that I have something in me that is no good. But it's not me who's no good. I'm not the sliver. The sliver that is stuck in my finger is no good. I am not sin and I am not a sinner. I am a saint who has allowed sin to reign in my mortal body, which causes me to do what I don't want to do.

On the Battleground

Verses 22 and 23 pinpoint the battleground for the contest between me and sin: "For in my inner being I delight in God's law; but I see another law at work in the members of my body, waging war against the law of my mind and making me a prisoner of the law of sin at work within my members" (*NIV*).

Where does my desire to do what's right come from? Paul uses the phrase "my inner being," referring to my new self where my spirit and God's Spirit are joined. This is the eternal part of me.

And where does sin attack me to keep me from doing what I really want to do? My flesh, my previously learned independence, continues to tempt me to rebel against God (see James 4:1). This is the temporary, earthly part of me. Where then do these two opponents wage war (see Galatians 5:17)? The battleground in my mind. That's why it is so important that we learn how to renew our minds (see Romans 12:2) and to take every thought captive to the obedience of Christ (see 2 Corinthians 10:5).

Paul finished his description of the contest between sin and the new self by saying, "What a wretched man I am! Who will rescue me from this body of death?" (Romans 7:24, *NIV*). Notice that he didn't say, "Sinful man that I am!" "Wretched" means "miserable," and there is no one more miserable than the person who wants to do right but can't. If we use our bodies as instruments of unrighteousness, we give the devil an opportunity in our lives, and he brings only misery.

The good news is: "Thanks be to God through Jesus Christ our Lord! . . . There is therefore now no condemnation for those who are in Christ Jesus" (Romans 7:25; 8:1). The battle for the mind is a winnable war, as we will see in the chapters ahead.

TRUTH ENCOUNTER

1. What does it mean to you to have a new nature as a believer?
2. Write a personal experience where you gained victory over the flesh.
3. Where does the battle between you and sin occur?
4. What does "there is evil present in you, but it's not you" mean?

BECOMING THE SPIRITUAL PERSON YOU WANT TO BE

"Walking according to the Spirit is more like a relationship with a good friend than a list of dos and don'ts."

It was 1982 and the African country of Kenya was in turmoil. I (Dave) was returning to the United States after spending two and one-half months in Zaire as a short-term missionary. My plane had to stop in Kenya on the way home. As we landed, the pilot announced that rebel soldiers had attempted to overthrow the Kenyan government. The airport would be shut down indefinitely—from hours to perhaps days.

When I walked inside, the terminal was crawling with government soldiers carrying machine guns. The situation was tense to say the least. Fighting could break out again at any moment. It looked like a war zone!

As I sat in the airport, I looked into my small backpack and saw that I still had about 150 Swahili tracts. *These won't do me much good back home,* I thought. That's when I got into one of those silent arguments with God—you know, where the Holy Spirit jabs you in the ribs and tells you to start witnessing. I argued that I could get arrested or shot for witnessing. But I never was good at debating, especially with God.

So I grabbed a handful of the tracts and began to pass them out. But again God's voice whispered to my heart. "Don't just pass them out. *Tell* people the good news." I quietly submitted.

I approached two young Kenyan soldiers, thrust a small booklet toward them and asked if I could tell them about Jesus. To my surprise, they were very polite, seeming grateful to receive the booklet. Thankfully, they spoke English well, so I shared the gospel with them.

After going through the booklet, I asked the two soldiers if they would like to accept Christ as their Savior—right there.

I braced myself for the answer I've heard 100 times, the polite brush-off: "I'm sorry, I'm just not ready."

But instead, they smiled and said, "Yes." Then they put down their machine guns and bowed their heads. We prayed together there in the airport terminal. I was flooded with joy.

As soon as we finished praying, an officer approached and barked orders in Swahili. The two soldiers snapped to attention and hurried to obey the command. But as they left, both managed a glance my way. I saw more than a silent goodbye on their faces. There was the shine of thankfulness and joy.

I had just begun to compose myself when another soldier approached. "Have you been passing out tracts?" he asked. My heart skipped a few beats and then began to race. Everything in me wanted to say, "Who me? No way!" But I gathered my courage and said, "Yes I have." I just knew I was going to be arrested, thrown into prison, starved near to death, and then executed for passing out tracts.

"I am second in command of all these troops," the soldier said. "My men told me to come see you. They said they could see Christ in you."

My martyrdom would have to wait. Instead I was given the greatest compliment of my life: "We see Christ in you." My constant prayer is that Christ will be seen in me every day of my life.

What does it take to be a Christian in whom others can see Christ daily? What will move us away from selfishness and fleshly desires to loving service to God and others?

First, we need a firm grip on our identity in Christ. We can't love like Jesus loved until we accept the reality that, since we are in Christ, His divine nature is part of us.

Second, we must begin to put to death daily the old sin-trained flesh and live in harmony with who we are: children of God who are filled with God's Spirit.

Living out your true identity in Christ is called walking in the Spirit (see Galatians 5:16-18). How do we walk in the Spirit? Let's explore some of the guidelines in Scripture.

THREE PERSONS AND THE SPIRIT

In 1 Corinthians 2:14–3:3, Paul talks about three kinds of people: the spiritual person, the fleshly person and the natural person. The simple diagrams in this chapter will help you understand these three types of people and their differences.

THE NATURAL PERSON
LIFE "IN THE FLESH"
1 Corinthians 2:14

FLESH (Romans 8:8)
Though flesh can mean the body, it is the learned independence which gives sin its opportunity. The natural man who tries to find purpose and meaning in life independently of God is going to struggle with inferiority, insecurity, inadequacy, guilt, worry and doubts.

BODY
Tension or migraine headaches, nervous stomach, hives, skin rashes, allergies, asthma, some arthritis, spastic colon, heart palpitations, respiratory ailments, etc.

MIND
Obsessive thoughts, fantasty, etc.

EMOTIONS
Bitterness, anxiety, depression, etc.

WILL (Galatians 5:16-18)
Walk after the flesh:
immorality   jealousy
impurity   disputes
lustfulness   dissensions
idolatry   factions
witchcraft   envying
hatred   drunkenness
strife   carousing
outbursts of
 anger

SPIRIT
Man's spirit is dead to God (Ephesians 2:1-3); thus, the natural man is unable to fulfill the purpose for which he was created. Lacking life from God, sin is inevitable.

The Natural Person

Ephesians 2:1-3 gives us a good description of the natural person
Paul talks about in 1 Corinthians 2:14 (see Figure 5A). This person
is spiritually dead, separated from God, living independently from
God. The natural person can't help but sin.

The natural person has a soul, meaning he can think, feel and
choose. But as the arrows on the diagram show, his mind, emotions
and will are directed by his flesh, which acts completely apart from
the God who created him. The natural person may think he is free
to choose his behavior. But since he lives in the flesh, he can't help
but walk *according* to the flesh. His choices reflect the sinful activities listed in Galatians 5:19-21.

The natural person also has a body, of course. But he has no
spiritual resources for coping with the stresses of life or making
positive choices. So he may fall victim to one or more of the physical problems listed on the diagram. Having the peace of mind and
the calm assurance of God's presence in our lives positively affects
our physical health (see Romans 8:11).

The natural person's actions, reactions, habits and memories
are all controlled by the flesh, which encourages him to sinful
behavior. Because the sinful flesh is unchecked in his life, the natural person will struggle with feelings like "I'm a loser" (inferiority), "Nobody loves me" (insecurity), "I can't do anything right"
(inadequacy), as well as guilt, worry and doubt.

The Spiritual Person

The spiritual person has a body, soul and spirit. Yet, as shown in
Figure 5B, this person has been remarkably transformed from the
natural person he was before spiritual birth. When he accepted
Christ, his spirit was united with God's Spirit. He now enjoys forgiveness of sin, acceptance in God's family and the knowledge that
he is worth something.

The soul of the spiritual person shows the change that happened at spiritual birth. He now receives his power from the Spirit,
not from the flesh. His mind has been totally changed and made
new. His emotions are marked by peace and joy instead of turmoil.
And he is free to choose *not* to walk according to the flesh, but to
walk according to the Spirit. As the spiritual person chooses to
live in the Spirit, his life bears the fruit of the Spirit (see Galatians 5:22-23).

THE SPIRITUAL PERSON

LIFE "IN THE SPIRIT"
1 Corinthians 2:15

FLESH (Romans 8:8)
The crucifying of the flesh is the believer's responsibility, on a day-by-day basis as he considers himself dead to sin.

BODY
Temple of God (1 Corinthians 6:19-20)
Present as a living and holy sacrifice (Romans 12:1)

MIND
Transformed
(Romans 12:2)
Single-minded (Philippians 4:6-8)
Prepared for action
(1 Peter 1:13)

EMOTIONS
Peace (1 Colossians 3:15)
Joy (Philippians 4:4)

WILL (Galatians 5:16-18)
Walk after the Spirit:
love
joy
peace
kindness
goodness
faithfulness
gentleness
self-control

SPIRIT (Romans 8:9)
Salvation (John 3:3; 1 John 3:9)
Forgiveness (Acts 2:38; Hebrews 8:12)
Assurance (Romans 8:16)
Security (Ephesians 1:13-14)
Accepted (1 John 3:1)
Worth (Ephesians 2:10)

The body of the spiritual person has also been changed. It is now a place where the Holy Spirit lives. The spiritual person offers his body as a living sacrifice of worship and service to God. The flesh, which was trained to live without God under the old self, is still there in the spiritual person. But he obediently puts to death the flesh and its desires daily. He considers himself dead to the sin that tempts him with bad choices.

"That all looks and sounds great," you may say. "But *I'm* a Christian and I still have some problems. Sometimes I think the wrong kinds of thoughts—like about the opposite sex. Sometimes I do things that are from the natural person's list—like lie to my parents, cheat on a homework assignment, use hateful language toward someone. I'm far from being the spiritual person in the diagram."

Don't be discouraged. The description of the spiritual person is a picture of us at our best. It's what we would all look like if we were completely mature in Christ and always made the right choices (see 2 Peter 1:3). But most of us live somewhere on the slope between this mountaintop of being grown up spiritually and the childlike fleshly behavior described in Figure 5C. As you walk by the Spirit, understand that you *are* growing up and becoming more like the ideal model of the spiritual person every day.

The Fleshly Person
Notice that the spirit of the fleshly person is the same as that of the spiritual person. The fleshly person is a Christian, spiritually alive in Christ and declared righteous by God. But that's where the similarity ends. Instead of being directed and controlled by the Spirit, this believer chooses to follow the temptations of his flesh. As a result, his mind is full of sinful thoughts and he has a lot of negative emotions. And although he is free to walk in the Spirit and produce fruit, he chooses to get involved in sinful activity by doing what his flesh suggests.

His physical body is a temple of God in bad shape. He often has the same troubling physical problems that the natural person has because he is not living the way God created him to live. He is not presenting his body to God as a worshipful sacrifice. Instead he does whatever his physical desires demand. Since he gives in to the flesh instead of putting it to death, the fleshly person also battles feelings of inferiority, insecurity, inadequacy, guilt, worry and doubt.

FIGURE 5C

THE FLESHLY PERSON
LIFE "ACCORDING TO THE FLESH"
1 Corinthians 3:3

FLESH (Romans 8:8)
The ingrained habit
patterns still appeal
to the mind to live
independently of God.

BODY
Tension or migraine headaches, nervous
stomach, hives, skin rashes, allergies,
asthma, some arthritis, spastic colon, heart
palpitations, respiratory ailments, etc.

MIND
Double-minded

WILL (Galatians 5:16-18)
Walk after the Spirit (seldom):
love   joy   self-control
kindness   peace   patience
gentleness goodness faithfulness

EMOTIONS
Unstable

SPIRIT (Romans 8:9)
Alive but quenched
(1 Thessalonians 5:19)

WILL (Galatians 5:16-18)
Walk after the flesh (often):
immorality strife   impurity
jealousy   lustfulness   disputes
idolatry   dissensions witchcraft
factions   hatred   envying
outbursts   drunkenness carousing
 of anger

Why are so many believers living so far below their potential in Christ? Why are so few of us enjoying the abundant, productive life we have inherited?

Part of the answer is related to how we grow and mature as Christians. In order to enjoy the benefits of the spiritual person, each one of us must remember who we are in Christ and actively apply that truth to our daily walk. We can't drift lazily along as Christians and expect to live victoriously over the flesh and sin.

Another part of the answer is that we don't realize how much the kingdom of darkness effects how we grow and mature. We have a living, personal enemy—Satan—who constantly tries to block our growth and maturity as God's children. We must know how to stand against him.

We sometimes live as though Satan and his dark and shadowy realm don't exist. And our ignorance in this area is crippling our freedom in Christ. We will talk more about Satan's plan of attack and how he tries to set up strongholds in our minds in chapter 9.

GUIDELINES FOR THE SPIRIT-FILLED WALK

If you are hoping for a magic formula or a list of foolproof steps for walking in the Spirit, you will be disappointed. Walking according to the Spirit is more like a relationship with a good friend than a list of dos and don'ts.

When two people first meet, the conversation is usually pretty shallow. But after you have been friends for several months or years, you know the person well and talk together easily. Walking in the Spirit is the process of getting to know God more and more and learning to trust Him as He helps you grow into the spiritual person you want to be.

Even though Scripture doesn't give us a formula, it does help us see what the Spirit-filled walk is and what it is *not*. Galatians 5:16-18 is a good place to start:

> Walk by the Spirit, and you will not carry out the desire of the flesh. For the flesh sets its desire against the Spirit, and the Spirit against the flesh; for these are in opposition to one another, so that you may not do the things that you please. But if you are led by the Spirit, you are not under the Law.

What the Spirit-filled Walk Is Not

You may see that last phrase, "You are not under the Law," and exclaim, "Wow, I'm free! Walking in the Spirit means I can do anything I want!"

Not at all. That's called license, a total disregard for God's loving guidelines. Being led by the Spirit means you are free to do the right thing and to live a responsible life—something you couldn't do when you were the prisoner of your flesh.

Once I (Neil) was invited to speak to a religion class at a Catholic high school on the topic of Protestant Christianity. At the end of my talk, an athletic-looking, street-wise student raised his hand and asked, "Do you have a lot of don'ts in your church?"

Sensing that he had a deeper motive, I answered, "What you really want to ask me is if we have any freedom, right?" He nodded.

"Sure, I'm free to do whatever I want to do," I answered.

His face mirrored his disbelief.

"Get serious," he said.

"Sure," I said. "I'm free to rob a bank. But I'm wise enough to realize that I would be in bondage to that act for the rest of my life. I'd have to cover up my crime, go into hiding or eventually pay for what I did. I'm also free to do drugs, get drunk and live a sexually immoral lifestyle. All of those 'freedoms' lead to bondage. I'm free to make those choices, but considering the consequences, would I really be free?"

What appears to be freedom to some people isn't really freedom but a return to bondage (see Galatians 5:1). God's laws are designed to protect you, not tie you down and strangle you. Your real freedom is your ability to choose to live obediently within the protective guidelines God has made for our lives.

Walking by the Spirit is also not obeying a bunch of rules. Trying to make ourselves spiritual by following Christian dos and don'ts will only result in defeat (see 2 Corinthians 3:6). When your mom or dad tells you not to do something, what do you immediately want to do? Cross that line!

Laying down the law—telling someone that it is wrong to do this or that—does not give them the power to stop doing it. Paul said that the law actually increases the desire to do what it says is wrong (see Romans 7:5)!

And neither can you produce a Spirit-filled heart by demanding that people do good things. Christian practices such as Bible study, prayer, regular church attendance and witnessing are not equal to spiritual maturity. All these activities are good and essential for spiritual growth. But merely doing these activities does not guarantee a Spirit-filled walk.

Does this mean that rules for behavior in the Bible are bad? Of course not. God's law is a necessary, protective standard and guideline. Within God's law we are free to develop a spirit-to-Spirit relationship with God (see 2 Corinthians 3:5-6).

What the Spirit-filled Walk Is

The Spirit-filled walk is neither license—doing anything we want—nor legalism—strict rules and regulations—but liberty, the freedom to be who we already are in Christ: loved, accepted children of God (see 2 Corinthians 3:6,17).

Our freedom in Christ is one of the most precious gifts we have received from God. You no longer have to walk according to the flesh as you did before you received Christ. You are not even forced to walk according to the Spirit. You can choose to walk according to the Spirit or to walk according to the flesh.

Walking according to the Spirit implies two things. First, we're talking about walking in the Spirit, not sitting in the Spirit. Putting our mind in neutral and coasting as Christians is dangerous and harmful to our spiritual growth. We must stay alert and active as believers. Second, we're talking about walking in the Spirit, not running in the Spirit. The Spirit-filled life is not achieved through endless, exhausting activity. We mistakenly think that the harder we work for God, the more spiritual we will become. That's a lie from the enemy. Satan knows that he may not be able to stop you from serving God by making you immoral. But he can probably slow you down by simply making you too busy.

Matthew 11:28-30 contains a neat description of the purpose and pace of the Spirit-filled walk. Jesus said, "Come to Me, all who are weary and heavy-laden, and I will give you rest. Take My yoke upon you, and learn from Me, for I am gentle and humble in heart; and you shall find rest for your souls. For My yoke is easy, and My load is light."

Jesus invites you to a restful walk with Him, just as two oxen walk together under the same yoke. "How can a yoke be restful?" you ask. Because Jesus' yoke is an easy yoke. As the lead ox, Jesus walks at a steady pace. If you pace yourself with Him, your burden will be easy.

The picture of walking in the Spirit together with Jesus also helps us understand our service to God. How much will you get done without Jesus pulling on His side of the yoke? Nothing. And how much will be accomplished without you on your side? Nothing. God has chosen to work in partnership with you to do His work in the world today.

Walking by Being Led

Walking according to the Spirit is also a matter of being led by the Spirit (see Romans 8:14). That's why the Lord pictures our relationship with Him in Scripture as a shepherd and his sheep.

Those of us who live in the Western world don't have a correct picture of what it means to be led like sheep. Western shepherds drive their sheep from behind the flock, often using dogs to bark at their heels. Eastern shepherds, like those in Bible times, lead their sheep from in front. When a shepherd is ready to leave the pasture, he gets up, says a few words to the sheep and walks away—and the sheep follow him! It's just like the words of Jesus in John 10:27: "My sheep hear My voice, and I know them, and they follow Me."

The Spirit-filled walk is one of being led, not driven. If you ever feel an inner push inside to do something you're not sure is right, it's probably not God leading you; it may be the devil driving you in the wrong direction. God *won't* make you walk in the Spirit, and the devil *can't* make you walk in the flesh, although he will certainly try to draw you in that direction. It is your choice to follow either the leading of the Spirit or the desires of the flesh.

The Proof Is in the Fruit

How can you know if you're being led by the Spirit or the flesh? Very simple: Look at your behavior. If you respond to a situation by exercising love, joy, peace, patience, kindness, goodness, faithfulness, gentleness and self-control, you are following the Spirit's lead (see Galatians 5:22-23). If you respond by doing something immoral, evil, hateful or viciously angry, you are walking according to the flesh (see Galatians 5:19-21). You are out of step with the lead ox, Jesus. You are either running ahead or dragging behind, straying off to the left or to the right. It shows that you need to draw closer to Jesus and learn from Him.

What do you do when you discover you are following the flesh instead of the Spirit? You admit it and correct it. Walking according to the Spirit is a moment-by-moment, day-by-day experience. When you step off the path of the Spirit, confess your sin to God and anyone you may have offended, receive forgiveness and return to walking the right path.

One Sunday morning when I (Neil) was a pastor, I told my family that we needed to leave for church at a certain time. When that time came, I was sitting in the car alone and starting to steam. Instead of taking the Spirit's path of love and patience, I was slowly turning off toward anger and resentment.

About two minutes later my wife and son came out. About five minutes later Heidi, my teenaged daughter, sauntered out. Instead of bringing her Bible, she had the latest issue of *Teen* magazine tucked under her arm.

"Get back in the house and get your Bible," I yelled harshly. I can't say that was the best Sunday morning I ever had. I had offended my family by my fleshly response and I needed to make it right.

We came home after church and sat down together for dinner. "Before we pray," I said, "I need to ask your forgiveness. I blew up before church. I was wrong." They forgave me and the relationship was restored.

"If I have to confess every time I offend someone," you may say, "I'll be confessing all the time." Yes, we are saints who sin by making wrong choices. And it may be humbling to confess all our failures. So here are a couple of things to consider when we are faced with making wrong things right.

First, we only need to confess to the people we have wronged. If you lash out at your little brother with angry words, you need only confess to God and your brother. You don't need to confess to your whole youth group or your pastor or your Bible study group.

If you hold on to a secret, lustful thought or proud attitude without hurting anyone else, you need only confess it to God. The only relationship affected is the one between you and Him.

Confession literally means to agree with God. When you realize that you have sinned, quickly confess it. Then mentally ask the Lord to fill you with His Spirit and get back in step with Christ.

Second, the process of getting right with others through confession and forgiveness is a step of spiritual growth. Your role as a friend, big brother or sister, or fellow-Christian is to model growth, not perfection. You are not perfect—and everyone around you knows it! If you're trying to keep up a front of Christian perfection in order to encourage others, forget it; it will never happen. But when you openly admit and ask forgiveness for your fleshly choices, you model the kind of spiritual growth that will touch many people.

Walking according to the Spirit is a freedom issue. You are free to choose to follow the flesh or the Spirit. But beware: Satan is not happy about you being free. He will try every deceptive trick he can devise to keep you from realizing and enjoying the liberty you have been given in Christ.

It's like a baby elephant captured for the circus and chained to a small tree. The little creature is too small to break the chain or uproot the tree. But when it grows, tripling in size and strength, it's strong enough to break away from the chain and the tree. But it doesn't because it's been programmed to captivity. It remembers trying and failing to escape as a calf. Now it no longer tries, even though it is strong enough to break free.

In Christ we are free from the power of sin. But if Satan can convince us that we're not free, just like the big elephant, we will remain in captivity when we could be walking free. The more you walk in step with Jesus and learn of Him, the better prepared you will be to recognize Satan's deception and disarm his strategy.

TRUTH ENCOUNTERS

1. How does "doing your own thing" lead to bondage, and how does living a responsible life ensure our freedom?
2. In what ways have you experienced God's protection through His laws?
3. Why are so many believers living below their potential in Christ?
4. In what ways are you tempted to sit back or run ahead of God?

THE POWER OF POSITIVE BELIEVING

*"With the all-powerful of the universe as the object of
Christian faith, there's hardly any limit to the spiritual heights
that positive believing can take you."*

Faith—we hear that word all the time in youth group meetings and
at church. Sometimes we hear people outside the church talk
about faith: "Have faith in yourself"; "Keep the faith"; "If you just
have faith, everything will work out all right." It seems that everyone has an idea about what faith is.

In the classic adventure film *Indiana Jones and the Last Crusade*,
filmmakers Steven Spielberg and George Lucas dramatized one version of faith. In the story, Indiana Jones was searching for the myth-
ical Holy Grail, the cup Jesus supposedly drank from at the Last
Supper. In order to reach the grail, Jones had to solve three potentially fatal clues prepared to test the skill and faith of treasure hunters.

Indy solved the first clue just in time to avoid being sliced in
half by two huge blades. Before he figured out the second clue, a
mistake almost dropped him thousands of feet to his death. But he
corrected his error in the nick of time and moved closer to his prize.

In the final challenge, Indiana Jones had to make a "leap of
faith." He came to a deep, impassable chasm. The Holy Grail wait-
ed for him on the other side. The clue directed Indy to step from
the cliff for an unbroken fall into a deep chasm. After hesitating,
he took a deep breath and stepped off the ledge for what appeared
to be a long, deadly fall. But instead, after only a few feet, he landed on a pathway of stone, unseen from the ledge above, which led
across the chasm to the treasure. His leap of faith into nothingness paid off.

Faith is vital to the Christian life. The author of Hebrews
summed it up by writing, "Without faith it is impossible to please

Him, for he who comes to God must believe that He is, and that He is a rewarder of those who seek Him" (Hebrews 11:6). Believing who God is, what He says and what He does is the passkey into the kingdom of God.

Furthermore, faith is central to everything we do as Christians. Paul wrote, "As you therefore have received Christ Jesus the Lord, so walk in Him" (Colossians 2:6). How did we receive Christ? By faith. How then are we to walk in Him? By faith. In Scripture, walking refers to the way we live our everyday lives. The Christian's daily success at spiritual growth and maturity hinges on walking by faith in Christ. Trusting in what God has done for us and who we are in Christ is the basis for growing up in Christ.

But what is faith? Is it a blind leap into nothingness as in the Indiana Jones film? As Christians, does God demand that we believe in Him without any evidence at all that He is worthy of our trust? Not at all. God doesn't ask us to take a blind leap. He has given us evidence that clearly shows He is worthy of our complete trust. Jesus became a man and lived among us. He was a real person, a historical figure. People who lived near Him could see and touch Him.

Furthermore, God told us about Jesus and what He would be like thousands of years before He came. God gave us specific prophecies in the Bible—more than 300 of them that were perfectly fulfilled by Christ the Messiah. God told us where and when Jesus would be born and how He would die. To top it all off, Jesus did something only God could do: He came back from the dead and is alive today. Our faith is firmly based on the solid evidence of the life of Jesus Christ and the truth of God's Word.

THE DIMENSIONS OF DOWN-TO-EARTH FAITH

We tend to think of faith as some kind of mystical quality that belongs in the realm of the spiritual, not in the practical, nuts-and-bolts area of everyday living. But faith is more concrete than you may realize. Here are three simple aspects of faith that will bring it out of the mysterious and into the practical side of life.

1. Faith Depends on Its Object
Faith is not simply a matter of believing. It's *what* we believe and *who* we believe in that determines whether or not our faith will be

rewarded. Everybody walks by faith every day. Every time you borrow the car from Mom or Dad and drive on the highway, you do so by faith. When you approach a green light, you drive through it believing that the drivers facing the red light will stop, even though you can't see the red light. If you didn't believe they would see the red light and stop, you wouldn't go through the intersection without slowing down to make sure no one was about to run the red light.

Are the objects of our faith on the highway reliable? Most of the time they are because most drivers drive safely. But you or a friend may have been involved in an accident by placing faith in another driver who at that moment proved to be unworthy of that trust.

What happens when the object of our faith fails us? We give up on it—maybe not immediately, but how many failures do we put up with before saying, "Never again!" Once faith is damaged or lost, it is very difficult to regain. Our belief isn't the problem; it's the object of our belief that either rewards or destroys our faith. If a steady boyfriend or girlfriend dumps you, or a friend or relative hurts you badly, your faith in that person is weak because he or she did not live up to your trust. When faith in a person is shattered, it takes months or years to rebuild.

Some faith-objects, however, are solid. You set your watch, plan your calendar and schedule your day believing that the earth will continue to revolve around the sun at its current speed. If the earth's orbit shifted just a few degrees, our lives would be turned to chaos. But so far, the laws governing the physical universe have been among the most trustworthy faith-objects we have.

The ultimate focal point or faith-object, of course, is not the sun, but the Son: "Jesus Christ is the same yesterday and today, yes and forever" (Hebrews 13:8). It is the fact that Jesus never changes that makes Him so trustworthy (see Numbers 23:19; Malachi 3:6). He has never failed to do all that He said He would do and be all that He said He would be. He is eternally faithful.

2. Faith Is Determined by the Depth of Knowledge of the Object

When people struggle with their faith in God, it's not because God is insufficient. It's because what they know about God is insufficient. They expect Him to operate in a certain way or answer prayer a certain way—their way, not His. When He doesn't comply, they say, "Forget You, God." But God doesn't change; He's the perfect focal point for our faith. Faith in God only fails when people misunderstand God and His ways.

If you want your faith in God to grow, you must increase your understanding of Him as the object of your faith. If you have little knowledge about God and His Word, you will have little faith. If you have great knowledge about God and His Word, you will have great faith. Faith cannot be pumped up by coaxing yourself, "If only I can believe! If only I can believe!" Any attempt to push yourself beyond what you know about God and His ways is to move from real faith to the blind faith Indiana Jones displayed. The only way to increase your faith is to increase your knowledge of God. That's why Paul wrote, "Faith comes from hearing, and hearing by the word of Christ" (Romans 10:17).

"Well," you may say, "that means there's a limit to our faith." Yes, there's a limit. But God isn't controlling it—you are. As the object of our faith, He is unlimited. The only limit to our faith is our knowledge and understanding of God. That knowledge grows every time we read the Bible, memorize a new Scripture verse, participate in a Bible study or meditate on a scriptural truth. Can you see the practical potential for your faith to grow as you seek to know and believe God through His Word? It's boundless!

3. Faith Is an Action Word

When my son Karl was just a toddler, I (Neil) would stand him up on the table and call for him to jump from the table into my arms. Did Karl believe that I would catch him? Yes. How did I know he believed? Because he jumped. Suppose he wouldn't jump. "Do you believe I will catch you, Karl?" I might ask, and he may nod yes. But if he never jumps, does he really believe that I will catch him? No. Faith involves action. Faith takes a stand. Faith makes a move. Faith speaks up.

There are a lot of Christians who claim to have great faith in God, but who are spiritual couch potatoes who don't do anything. Faith without action is not faith: It's dead, meaningless (see James 2:17-18). If it isn't expressed, it isn't faith. In order to believe God and His Word, we must do what He says. If we don't do what He says, we don't really believe and trust Him. Faith and action are inseparable.

Sadly, one of the common pictures of the Church today is of a group of people with an assumed faith but little action. We're thankful that our sins are forgiven and that Jesus is preparing a place in heaven for us, but we're basically cowering in fear and defeat in the world, just hanging on until the rapture. We treat the Church as if it's a hospital. We get together to compare wounds and hold each other's hands, yearning for Jesus to come take us away.

But is that the picture of the Church in the New Testament? No way! The Church is not a hospital; it's a military outpost under orders to storm the gates of hell. Every believer is on active duty, called to take part in fulfilling the Great Commission (see Matthew 28:19-20). Thankfully the Church has an infirmary where we can minister to the weak and wounded, and that ministry is necessary. But we don't exist for that. Our real purpose is to be change agents in the world, taking a stand, living by faith and accomplishing something for God. We can say we believe God and His Word, but if we are not actively involved in His cause, we don't believe.

THE MAN WHO THINKS HE CAN

If you think you are beaten, you are;
If you think you dare not, you don't.
If you'd like to win, but think you can't,
It's almost a cinch you won't.
If you think you'll lose, you're lost.
For out of the world we find
Success begins with a fellow's will;
It's all in the state of mind. . . .
Life's battles don't always go
To the stronger or faster man;
But soon or late the man who wins
Is the one who thinks he can.[1]

This poem reflects the popular view of life known as the power of positive thinking. Christians are somewhat reluctant to buy into this view, and for good reason. For example, you can think as positively as you want that you don't need oxygen to live. But no amount of positive thinking is going to keep you from drowning if you're trapped under water for more than just a few minutes.

The Christian, however, has far greater potential for success in life in the power of positive *believing*. Faith uses our ability to think but is not limited by it. Faith actually goes beyond the limitations of the mind and uses the real, but unseen, world. The believer's faith is as valid as its object, which is the living and written Word of God—Jesus Christ and the Bible. With the all-powerful God of the universe as the object of Christian faith, there's hardly any limit to the spiritual heights that positive believing can take you.

Someone has said that success comes in cans and failure in cannots. Believing that we can succeed at Christian growth and maturity takes no more effort than believing we cannot succeed. So why not believe that we can walk in faith and in the Spirit, that we can resist the temptations of the world, the flesh and the devil, and that we can grow to maturity as a Christian. The following Twenty Cans of Success, taken from God's Word, will expand your knowledge of our faith-object, the Almighty God. Building your faith by storing these paraphrased truths in your heart will lift you from the quicksand of the cannots to sit with Christ in the heavenlies:

TWENTY CANS OF SUCCESS

1. Why should I say I can't when the Bible says I can do all things through Christ who gives me strength (see Philippians 4:13)?
2. Why should I worry about my needs when I know that God will take care of all my needs according to His riches in glory in Christ Jesus (see Philippians 4:19)?
3. Why should I fear when the Bible says God has not given me a spirit of fear, but of power, love and a sound mind (see 2 Timothy 1:7)?
4. Why should I lack faith to live for Christ when God has given me plenty of faith (see Romans 12:3)?
5. Why should I be weak when the Bible says that the Lord is the strength of my life and that I will display strength and take action because I know God (see Psalm 27:1; Daniel 11:32)?
6. Why should I allow Satan control over my life when He that is in me is greater than he that is in the world (see 1 John 4:4)?

7. Why should I accept defeat when the Bible says that God always leads me in victory (see 2 Corinthians 2:14)?

8. Why should I lack wisdom when I know that Christ became wisdom to me from God and God gives wisdom to me generously when I ask Him for it (see 1 Corinthians 1:30; James 1:5)?

9. Why should I be depressed when I can recall to mind God's lovingkindness, compassion and faithfulness and have hope (see Lamentations 3:21-23)?

10. Why should I worry and be upset when I can cast all my problems on Christ who cares for me (see 1 Peter 5:7)?

11. Why should I ever be in bondage knowing that there is freedom where the Spirit of the Lord is (see Galatians 5:1)?

12. Why should I feel condemned when the Bible says I won't be condemned because I am in Christ (see Romans 8:1)?

13. Why should I feel alone when Jesus said He is with me always and He will never leave me nor forsake me (see Matthew 28:20; Hebrews 13:5)?

14. Why should I feel like I'm cursed or have bad luck when the Bible says that Christ rescued me from the curse of the law that I might receive His Spirit (see Galatians 3:13-14)?

15. Why should I be unhappy when I, like Paul, can learn to be satisfied in all kinds of conditions (see Philippians 4:11)?

16. Why should I feel worthless when Christ became sin for me so that I might become acceptable to God (see 2 Corinthians 5:21)?

17. Why should I feel that others are out to get me when I know that nobody can be against me when God is for me (see Romans 8:30)?

18. Why should I be confused when God is the author of peace and He gives me knowledge through His Spirit who lives in me (see 1 Corinthians 2:12; 14:33)?

19. Why should I feel like a failure when I am a conqueror in all things through Christ (see Romans 8:37)?

20. Why should I let the pressures of life bother me when I can take courage knowing that Jesus has overcome the world and its problems (see John 16:33)?

WHAT HAPPENS WHEN I STUMBLE IN MY WALK OF FAITH?

Have you ever felt that God is ready to give up on you because, instead of walking in faith, you sometimes stumble and fall? Do you ever fear that there is a limit to what God will put up with and you're sure you have crossed the line of His love? A lot of Christians live like that. They think that God is upset with them, that He is ready to dump them or that He has already given up on them because their daily performance is less than perfect.

It's true that we sometimes interrupt our walk of faith and have moments of unbelief or rebellion or even satanic deception. It's during those moments when we think that God has surely lost His patience with us and is ready to give up on us. And how do some respond when they suspect that God has given up? They give up too. They stop walking by faith altogether, slump dejectedly by the side of the road and wonder, *What's the use?* They feel defeated, God's work for them stops and Satan loves it.

God Loves You Just the Way You Are

The important truth you need to know about God in order for your faith to remain strong is that His love and acceptance is not based on what you do or don't do. God's love for you is eternal; it never ends. When your walk of faith is strong, God loves you. When your walk of faith is weak, God loves you. When you're strong one moment and weak the next, strong one day and weak the next, God loves you. God's love for you is the same no matter how good or bad you are doing in your daily walk.

When Mandy came to see me (Neil), she appeared to have her life all together. She was a Christian who was very active in her church. She had led her alcoholic father to Christ on his deathbed. She was pretty and she had a nice husband and two wonderful children. But she had attempted suicide at least three times.

"How can God love me?" Mandy sobbed. "I'm such a failure, such a mess."

"Mandy, God loves you, not because you are lovable, but because it is His nature to love you. God simply loves you—period, because God is love."

"But when I do bad, I don't feel like God loves me," she argued.

"Don't trust those feelings. He loves all His children all the time, whether we do good or bad. That's the heart of God. When the 99 sheep were safe in the fold, the heart of the shepherd was with the 1 that was lost. When the prodigal son spent his life and inheritance, the heart of his father was with him, and he lovingly welcomed his son home. Those parables show us that God's heart is full of love for us."

"But I've tried to take my own life, Neil. How can God overlook that?"

"Just suppose, Mandy, that your son became so depressed that he tried to take his own life. Would you love him any less? Would you kick him out of the family? Would you turn your back on him?"

"Of course not. If anything I'd feel sorry for him and try to love him more."

"Are you telling me that a perfect God isn't as good a parent to you as you, an imperfect person, are to your children?"

Mandy got the point. She began to realize that God, as a loving parent, can overlook weaknesses and forgive sin.

God Loves You No Matter What You Do

God wants us to do good, of course. The apostle John wrote, "I write this to you so that you will not sin." But John continued by reminding us that God has already made provision for our failure so that His love continues constant in spite of what we do:

> But if anybody does sin, we have one who speaks to the Father in our defense—Jesus Christ, the Righteous One. He is the atoning sacrifice for our sins, and not only for ours but also for the sins of the whole world (1 John 2:1-2, *NIV*).

One reason we doubt God's love is that we have an adversary, the devil, who uses every little offense to accuse us of being good-for-nothings. But your advocate—your defender, Jesus Christ—is more powerful than your adversary. He has cancelled the debt of your sins past, present and future. No matter what you do or how you fail, God has no reason not to love you and accept you completely.

God wants you to accept your identity in Him and live as a child of God should. But even when you forget who you are, He still loves you. He wants you to walk in the Spirit and in faith. But even when you stumble off the path, He still loves you.

TRUTH ENCOUNTER

1. Who is the object of your faith?
2. Why do you need to really know your faith object?
3. Why is action so important to real faith?
4. How does God feel about you when you stumble in your walk of faith? What would that cause you to do when you do stumble?

Note

1. Walter D. Wintle, "The Man Who Thinks He Can," quoted in Hazel Felleman, comp., *Poems That Live Forever* (New York: Doubleday, 1965), p. 310.

YOU CAN'T LIVE BEYOND WHAT YOU BELIEVE

*"Your Christian walk is the direct result of
what you believe about God and yourself.
If your faith is off, your walk will be off."*

When my son Karl was about 10 years old, I (Neil) introduced him
to the game of golf. I gave him a little starter set of clubs and took
him out to the course with me. Karl would tee up his ball and whale
away at it with his mightiest swing. Usually he sprayed the ball all
over the place. But since he could only hit it 60 or 70 yards at best,
his direction could be off by 15 degrees or so and his ball would still
be on the fairway.

As he grew up and got a bigger set of clubs, Karl was able to
drive the ball off the tee 150 yards and farther. But if his drive was
still 15 degrees off target, his ball no longer stayed in the fairway; it
usually went onto the rough. Accuracy is even more important for
golfers who can blast a golf ball 200 to 250 yards off the tee. The
same 15 degrees that allowed little Karl's short drives to remain on
the fairway will send a longer drive soaring out of bounds.

This simple illustration pictures an important aspect of the life
of faith: Your Christian walk is the direct result of what you believe
about God and yourself. If your faith is off, your walk will be off. If
your walk is off, you can be sure it's because your faith is off.

As new Christians, we needed some time to learn how to "hit
the ball straight" in our belief system. We could be off 15 degrees
in what we believed and still be on the fairway because we were
still growing and had a lot to learn. But the longer we hold on to
a poor belief system, the less fulfilling and productive our daily
walk of faith will be.

Some Christians believe that walking by faith means being car-
ried along by a mysterious, indescribable, inner sense called faith—

kind of like "the force" in the *Star Wars* movies. But the walk of faith is much more practical and real than that. Walking by faith simply means that we function in daily life on the basis of what we believe. In fact, we already walk by faith; we can't *not* walk by faith. Our belief system determines our behavior. If our behavior is off in a certain area, we need to correct our belief in that area because our misbehavior is the result of our misbelief.

"But how can I know what I really believe?" you may ask. Here's a simple, two-part quiz that will help you identify your present belief system. Take a few minutes to complete the quiz. In Part One, rate yourself in each of the eight categories by circling a number from one to five that best represents you, five being high.

BELIEF QUIZ—PART ONE

	Low				High
1. How successful am I?	1	2	3	4	5
2. How significant am I?	1	2	3	4	5
3. How fulfilled am I?	1	2	3	4	5
4. How satisfied am I?	1	2	3	4	5
5. How happy am I?	1	2	3	4	5
6. How much fun am I having?	1	2	3	4	5
7. How secure am I?	1	2	3	4	5
8. How peaceful am I?	1	2	3	4	5

In Part Two, complete each of the eight statements as honestly as possible.

BELIEF QUIZ—PART TWO

1. I would be more successful if _____

2. I would be more significant if _____

3. I would be more fulfilled if _____

4. I would be more satisfied if _____

5. I would be happier if _____

6. I would have more fun if _____

7. I would be more secure if _____

8. I would have more peace if _____

Whatever you believe is the answer to the above questions makes up your present belief system. Assuming that your basic needs for food, shelter, safety and so forth are met, you will be motivated in life by what you believe will bring you success, significance, fulfillment, satisfaction, happiness, fun, security and peace. And if what you believe about these eight values does not line up with what God says about them in His Word, your walk of faith will be off to the same degree that your belief is off.

FEELINGS ARE GOD'S RED FLAG OF WARNING

God desires all His children to experience success, significance, fulfillment, satisfaction, happiness, fun, security and peace. From birth we have been figuring out the best ways to experience these eight values and reach other goals in life. Whether we think about it or not, we continue to figure and adjust our plans for reaching these goals.

But sometimes our well-intended plans and noble-sounding goals are not completely in harmony with God's plans and goals for us. *How can I know if what I believe is right?* you may be wondering. *Do I have to wait until I am out of college or old and gray to discover that what I believed in these eight areas was wrong?* No, you don't have to wait.

God has designed you in such a way that you can know on a moment-by-moment basis if your belief system is properly lined up with God's truth. God can grab your attention so that you can know if you have a good goal or a bad goal. He uses your emotions. When someone or something leaves you feeling angry, anxious or depressed, those emotional signposts are there to alert you that you may be holding on to a poor goal, which is based on a wrong belief. Though emotions will change, and may not always be 100 percent reliable, they are designed to alert us to poor goals or faulty beliefs.

Anger Signals a Blocked Goal

When you're feeling angry about a relationship or a project, it's usually because someone or something has blocked your goal. Any goal that can be blocked by forces you can't control (other than God) is not a healthy goal, because your success is out of your hands.

For example, you may say, "My goal in life is to have a loving, happy family all the time." Who can block that goal? Every person in your family can block that goal—not only *can*, they *will*. If you're clinging to the belief that your happiness is dependent on your family, you'll crash and burn every time your dad or mom or brother or sister fails to live up to your image of family harmony. You will probably be a very angry person, which could drive family members even farther away from you and each other.

Feelings of anger warn us to reexamine what we believe and the goals we have put together.

Anxiety Signals an Uncertain Goal

Anxiety is that uneasy feeling inside us—kind of like worry and fear mixed together—that comes when we're not sure what's going to happen. When we feel anxious in an activity or relationship, our anxiety may be signaling that we're not sure about the goal we have chosen. We hope something will happen, but we have no guarantee that it will. We can control some of the factors, but not all of them, so worry begins to chew at our insides.

For example, you may believe that your happiness depends on your parents allowing you to attend a concert by a hot new rock group. Not knowing how they will respond, you get anxious. It's not a Christian group, so you're a little nervous that they won't allow you to go. Your anxiety reveals the uncertainty of your goal.

If they say no, you'll be angry because your goal was blocked. But what if you know all along that your parents will say something like, "A non-Christian group? Not a chance!" You'll probably experience another emotion—depression—because your goal cannot be achieved

Depression Signals an Impossible Goal

When we base our future success on something that can never happen, we have an impossible, hopeless goal. Depression is a signal that our goal, no matter how spiritual or noble, may never be reached. Depression is the expression of hopelessness.

For example, let's say there is someone on your campus who is very out-going and always seems to have lots of friends. But you are shy and reserved with few friends. So you make up your mind that you are going to be just like that out-going person. You decide to change your personality and temperament so that you can be just like him or her.

Is that a good goal? No way! It's impossible to become exactly like someone else. If you base your happiness on a goal that's beyond your ability, depression will set in. Depression often signals that you are desperately clinging to a goal you have little or no chance of achieving, and that's not a healthy goal.

Sometimes the depression resulting from an impossible goal is related to a wrong concept of God. David wrote, "How long, O Lord? Will you forget me forever? How long will you hide your face from me? . . . How long will my enemy triumph over me?" (Psalm 13:1-2, *NIV*). Had God really forgotten David? Was He actually hiding from David? Of course not. David had a wrong concept of God, feeling that He had abandoned him to the enemy. David's wrong concept led him to an impossible goal: victory over his enemies without God's help. No wonder he felt depressed!

But the remarkable thing about David is that he didn't stay in the dumps. He looked over his situation and realized, "Hey, I'm a child of God. I'm going to focus on what I know about Him, not on my negative feelings." From the pit of his depression he wrote, "I trust in your unfailing love; my heart rejoices in your salvation" (Psalm 13:5, *NIV*). Then he decided to make a positive expression of his will: "I will sing to the Lord, for he has been good to me" (Psalm 13:6, *NIV*). He willfully moved away from his wrong concept and its accompanying depression and returned to the source of his hope.

If Satan can destroy your belief in God, you will lose your source of hope. But with God all things are possible. He is the source of all hope. You need to learn to respond to hopeless-appearing situations as David did: "Why are you in despair, O my soul? And why are you disturbed within me? Hope in God, for I shall again praise Him, the help of my countenance, and my God" (Psalm 43:5).

Wrong Responses to Those Who Frustrate Goals

When a person's happiness or success hinges on reaching a goal that can be blocked or that is uncertain or impossible, how will they respond to those who frustrate their goals? Often they will attempt to control or manipulate the people or circumstances that stand between them and their success.

For example, Darcy's goal is to win the last open spot on the cheerleading squad. But she learns that Brittany, one of her best friends, is trying out for the same spot. Brittany is far more popular and athletic, and Darcy knows her friend will easily beat her out for the vacant position. Darcy's goal is blocked. Her sense of self-worth and importance is on the line.

How does she feel about her best friend Brittany now? She's ticked. She's not sure she wants to be Brittany's friend anymore. Worse yet, she begins to look for underhanded ways to get Brittany out of the cheerleading picture. She attempts to influence the teachers who are making the final selection. She makes up lies about her friend, lies that could seriously damage Brittany's good reputation. She looks for ways to change Brittany's mind about trying out. Darcy insists, "I'll never be your friend again if you do this to me."

Why does she do all this? Because she believes that her significance and success depend on reaching her goal of making the cheerleading squad. A bad goal has created a bad situation between good friends.

People who cannot control those who frustrate their goals will probably respond by getting bitter, angry or resentful. They may simply resort to feeling sorry for themselves. Unless Darcy adjusts her goal, she will waste months and possibly years living in bitter defeat.

HOW CAN I TURN BAD GOALS INTO GOOD GOALS?

Here's a faith-stretching question: If God wants something done, can it be done? In other words, if God has a goal for your life, can it be blocked, or is its fulfillment uncertain or impossible?

Absolutely not. There is no goal that God has for your life that is impossible or uncertain, nor can it be blocked. Imagine God saying, "I've called you into existence, I've made you My child and I have something for you to do. I know you won't be able to do it, but give it your best shot." That's crazy! It's like your dad saying to you, "I want you to mow the lawn. Unfortunately, the lawn is full of rocks, the mower doesn't work and there's no gas. But give it your best shot."

God had a staggering goal for a girl named Mary. An angel told her that she would give birth to a son while still a virgin and that her son would be the Savior of the world. When she inquired about this seemingly impossible feat, the angel simply said, "Nothing will be impossible with God" (Luke 1:37).

Most parents don't give their children tasks they can't complete. God, our loving, perfect heavenly Father, doesn't assign us goals we can't achieve. His goals for us are possible, certain and achievable. The only requirement for success is your response. You must say with Mary, "Behold, the bondslave of the Lord; be it done to me according to your word" (Luke 1:38).

KNOWING THE DIFFERENCE BETWEEN GOALS AND DESIRES

The secret to achieving God's goals is learning the difference between a godly goal and a godly desire. This understanding can spell the difference between success and failure, inner peace and inner pain for the Christian.

A *godly goal* is any specific choice reflecting God's purposes for your life that does not depend on people or circumstances beyond your ability or right to control. Who do you have the ability and right to control? Virtually no one but yourself. The only person who can block a godly goal or render it uncertain or impossible is you. And if you adopt the attitude of cooperation with God's goals as Mary did, your goal can be reached.

A *godly desire* is any specific choice that depends on the cooperation of other people or the success of events or favorable circumstances you cannot control. You *cannot* base your self-worth or your personal success on your desires, no matter how godly they may be, because you cannot control their fulfillment. Some of your desires can be blocked, some are uncertain and some are impossible.

When a desire is wrongly treated as a goal and that goal is frustrated, you must deal with all the anger, anxiety and depression that may accompany that failure. But by comparison, when a desire isn't met, all you face is disappointment. Life is full of disappointments, and we all must learn to live with them. Dealing with the disappointments of unmet desires is a lot easier than dealing with the anger, anxiety and depression of goals that are based on wrong beliefs.

We must learn to distinguish between our goals and desires the way God does. For example, what does God say about sin? "My little children, I am writing these things to you that you may not sin"

(1 John 2:1). Certainly God desires that we don't sin, but is this a good goal as was defined earlier? It's not a goal because it can be blocked by anyone who exercises his will against repentance. But it is God's desire that everyone repent even though not everyone will.

Then does God have any genuine goals—specific results that cannot be blocked? Praise the Lord, *yes!* For example, Jesus Christ will return and take us home to heaven to be with Him forever—it will happen. Satan will be cast into the pit for eternity—count on it. Rewards will be distributed to the saints for their faithfulness— look forward to it. These are not desires that can be overcome by man's free will. What God has determined to do, He will do.

When you begin to align your goals with God's goals and your desires with God's desires, you will rid your life of a lot of anger, anxiety and depression. For example, Darcy will save herself a lot of grief if she changes her goal of making the cheerleading squad into a desire. Instead she could make it her goal to do her best during the tryouts and remain a good friend to Brittany no matter who is selected. She may have to deal with some disappointment, but those are godly goals no one can frustrate but Darcy.

GODLY GOALS CENTER ON BUILDING CHARACTER

God's basic goal for our lives is character development: becoming the persons He wants us to be. Because it's a godly goal, no one can block it except us. But there certainly are a lot of distractions, diversions, disappointments, trials, temptations and traumas that come along to disrupt the process. Every day we struggle against the world, the flesh and the devil, each of which is opposed to our success at being godly persons.

But Paul reminds us that the tough times we face are actually a means of achieving our supreme goal of maturity: "We also exult in our tribulations, knowing that tribulation brings about perseverance; and perseverance, proven character; and proven character, hope; and hope does not disappoint, because the love of God has been poured out within our hearts through the Holy Spirit who was given to us" (Romans 5:3-5). James offered similar encouragement: "Consider it all joy, my brethren, when you encounter various trials, knowing that the testing of your faith produces endurance. And let endurance have its perfect result, that you may be perfect and complete, lacking in nothing" (James 1:2-4).

Maybe you thought your goal as a Christian was to escape tough times. But God's goal for you is maturity in Christ, becoming the person He designed you to be. And tough times happen to be one of the primary stepping stones on the pathway. That's why Paul says we exult—meaning to express great joy—in our tribulations. Why? Because hanging in there during tough times is the doorway to proven character, which is God's goal for us.

Incidentally, committing yourself to hang in there and grow in a relationship problem leads to a win-win solution. Not only will you become a better person through the process, but it is by far the best way to win back a friend. You're so focused on becoming what God wants you to be in the relationship that you don't have time to try to change the other person or circumstance.

One of the great things about trials and tribulations in our lives is that they reveal wrong goals. Some kids say, "My family life is hopeless. My parents don't understand me and they're always on my back." So to solve the problem they run away from home. Others feel they have blown it at a certain school. So they change schools only to discover that the new school seems just as hopeless.

People tend to look for quick-fix solutions to difficult situations. But God's plan is for you to hang in there and grow up. Let the problem help you evaluate and adjust your goals and desires.

Isn't there an easier way to become the persons God wants us to be than by going through tough times? We're all looking for one. But it's the dark, difficult times of testing in our lives that bring us to the place where we learn that we can totally rely on God. We all need occasional mountaintop experiences. But the fertile soil for growth is always down in the valleys of tribulation, not on the mountain tops.

Paul says, "The goal of our instruction is love" (1 Timothy 1:5). If you make that your goal, then the result is joy, peace and patience (see Galatians 5:22) instead of the anger, anxiety and depression of frustrated goals.

TRUTH ENCOUNTER

1. What does anger in your life signal? What may need to change?
2. What is the difference between a goal and a desire?
3. What are some tribulations you've had in your life and what have you learned from them?
4. What is God's goal for your life?

GOD'S GUIDELINES FOR THE WALK OF FAITH

*"It is very important for our spiritual maturity
that our beliefs about success, importance,
fulfillment, satisfaction, happiness, fun, security
and peace are anchored in the Scriptures."*

My wife, Grace, and I (Dave) have a son named David, whom we often call "Davers." Like most Christian parents, we have prayed since he was born that God would make Davers into the Christlike person He wants him to be. But I had no idea what God was going to use to answer that prayer.

When Davers was four years old, he complained of a lot of pain in his legs and joints. We thought he was experiencing growing pains, but when we took him to the doctor the news was worse. Davers was diagnosed with rheumatoid arthritis, a painful disease that swells and deforms the hands, feet and joints in elderly people but is rare in children.

When we heard the news, I couldn't hold back my tears. The thought of our son living in such pain really shook me up. I couldn't see how rheumatoid arthritis could be any benefit to my son's growth into a godly man.

I remember many times when Davers woke me up in the middle of the night crying and calling to me, "Daddy, it hurts real bad." I would go to his room, pick him up in my arms and hold him. Davers would whimper, "Daddy, make the hurt go away, okay?" It broke my heart. I explained that I couldn't make the pain go away, but I could pray for him, which I always did.

In the months that followed, Grace and I noticed something very special happening to our son. He began to show a special sensitivity and compassion for others who were hurting. His daily pain developed a tenderness in him for others in pain.

I had no idea of the depth of his compassion until one night when I went to his room. Davers had been crying, and I said, "Are your legs hurting tonight, Davers?"

"No, Daddy," he replied. "I was just thinking about all the people who don't know Jesus, and it hurts my heart." His words blew me away.

Later I thought about our ongoing prayer for Davers to grow up to be a godly man. I realized that God was using rheumatoid arthritis to develop in Davers the Christlike heart of compassion Grace and I had been praying for all along. We just hadn't believed that such a bad thing could produce such a good result.

PROPER BELIEFS LEAD TO A PROPER WALK

As far as the devil is concerned, the next best thing to keeping us chained in spiritual darkness or having us live as emotional wrecks is confusing our belief system. He lost us in the eternal sense when we became children of God. But if he can muddy our minds and weaken our faith with partial truths, he can stop our effectiveness for God and stunt our growth as Christians if we let him.

We know that God wants us to be successful, fulfilled and happy. But it is very important for our spiritual maturity that our beliefs about success, importance, fulfillment, satisfaction, happiness, fun, security and peace are anchored in the Scriptures. I struggled with Davers's arthritis because my belief about his success, significance and fulfillment did not reflect scriptural truth.

In this chapter we will review each of these belief areas from the foundation of God's Word. Compare these eight descriptions with the eight statements you wrote on the Belief Quiz in the last chapter. These descriptions may help you make some important adjustments in your belief system, which will help you improve your daily walk with Christ.

1. Success Comes from Right Goals

Success in the Christian walk is directly related to our goals. If you ranked yourself low in the success category of the Belief Quiz, you are probably having difficulty reaching your goals in life. And if you aren't reaching your goals, it's probably because you're working on the wrong goals. A good summary of God's goal for us is found in 2 Peter 1:3-10:

His divine power has granted to us everything pertaining
to life and godliness, through the true knowledge of Him
who called us by His own glory and excellence. For by these
He has granted to us His precious and magnificent promises, in order that by them you might become partakers of
the divine nature, having escaped the corruption that is in
the world by lust.

Now for this very reason also, applying all diligence, in
your faith, supply moral excellence, and in your moral excellence, knowledge; and in your knowledge, self-control, and
in your self-control, perseverance, and in your perseverance,
godliness; and in your godliness, brotherly kindness, and in
your brotherly kindness, love. For if these qualities are
yours and are increasing, they render you neither useless
nor unfruitful in the true knowledge of our Lord Jesus
Christ. For he who lacks these qualities is blind or short-
sighted, having forgotten his purification from his former
sins. Therefore, brethren, be all the more diligent to make
certain about His calling and choosing you; for as long as
you practice these things, you will never stumble.

Notice that God's goal begins with who we are on the basis of
what God has already done for us. He has given us "life and godliness." Our sins have already been forgiven and we have been
declared righteous in Christ. We have already begun our growth to
maturity in Christ. Christ's divine nature is ours right now, and we
have escaped—that's past tense—sin's corruption. What a great
start! It happened the moment we accepted Christ.

Our primary job now is to diligently adopt God's character
goals—moral excellence, knowledge, self-control, perseverance,
godliness, brotherly kindness and Christian love—and apply them
to our lives. Focusing on God's goals will lead to ultimate success:
success in God's terms. Peter promises that, as these qualities
increase through practice, we will be useful and fruitful, and we
will never stumble. That's success!

Notice also that there is no mention in this list of talents, intelligence or gifts that are not equally distributed to all believers. Your
self-worth isn't determined by those qualities. Your self-worth is
based on your identity in Christ and your growth in character, both
of which are equally available to every Christian. Those Christians

who are not committed to God's goals for character are missing out on God's best for them. According to Peter, they have forgotten who they are. They are out of touch with their true identity and purpose in Christ.

Another helpful picture of success is seen in Joshua's experience of leading Israel into the Promised Land. God said to him:

> Be strong and very courageous; be careful to do according to all the law which Moses, My servant, commanded you; do not turn from it to the right or to the left, so that you may have success wherever you go. This book of the law shall not depart from your mouth, but you shall meditate on it day and night, so that you may be careful to do according to all that is written in it; for then you will make your way prosperous, and then you will have success (Joshua 1:7-8).

Was Joshua's success dependent on other people or circumstances? No way! Success hinged entirely on his obedience. If Joshua believed what God said and did what God told him to do, he would succeed. Sounds simple enough, but God immediately put Joshua to the test by giving him a rather strange battle plan for conquering Jericho. Marching around the city for seven days and then blowing a horn wasn't exactly an approved military tactic in Joshua's day!

But Joshua's success was conditional on obeying God regardless of how foolish His plan seemed. As Joshua 6 tells us, Joshua's success had nothing to do with the circumstances of the battle and everything to do with obedience. That should be your pattern too. Accept God's goal for your life and follow it obediently. You'll head straight to the bull's-eye of success by becoming the person God wants you to be. The only one who can keep you from that is you!

2. Significance Comes from Proper Use of Time
Significance is a time issue. What is forgotten as time passes is of little importance. What is remembered for eternity is of great importance. Paul wrote to the Corinthians: "If any man's work . . . remains, he shall receive a reward" (1 Corinthians 3:14). He told Timothy, "Discipline yourself for the purpose of godliness . . . since it holds promise for the present life and also for the life to come" (1 Timothy 4:7-8). If you want to increase your importance, focus your energies on really important activities: those that will remain for eternity.

Brian was the pastor of a small church. He also attended classes at the seminary where I (Neil) used to teach. He was in his mid-30s and married when he found out he had cancer. The doctors gave him less than two years to live.

One day Brian came to talk to me. "Ten years ago somebody gave a prophecy about me in church," he began. "They said I was going to do a significant work for God. I've led a few hundred people to Christ, but I haven't had a significant work for God yet. Do you think God is going to heal me so that the prophecy can be fulfilled?"

My mouth dropped open in shock. "You've led a few hundred people to Christ and don't think you have accomplished a great work for God? Brian, I know some big-name pastors in large churches who can't make that claim. I know some great Bible scholars who have probably never led anyone to Christ. If a few hundred people are believers today because of you, and they have influenced who knows how many other people for Christ, I'd call that a great work for God." (Brian is now with the Lord, having completed his significant ministry of reaching hundreds for Christ.)

We're in the important business of collecting treasures for eternity. What we do and say for Christ, no matter how unimportant it seems in this world, will last forever.

3. Fulfillment Comes from Serving Others

For the Christian, true fulfillment in life comes when we discover our unique gifts and abilities and use them to serve others and glorify the Lord. Peter said it this way: "As each one has received a special gift, employ it in serving one another" (1 Peter 4:10).

Some people mistakenly believe that our spiritual gifts aren't activated until we become mature adults. The Bible doesn't teach that. If you have accepted Christ, the Holy Spirit is living in you and you have at least one spiritual gift. Age and maturity will help you discover and nurture your gifts, but they have nothing to do with receiving spiritual gifts.

God has a unique place of ministry for each of us. It is important to your sense of fulfillment that you realize exactly where that place is. The key is to discover the roles you occupy in which you cannot be replaced, and then decide to be what God wants you to be in those roles. For example, of the more than 6 billion people in the world, you are the only one who occupies your unique role in your home. God has specially planted you to serve Him by being the best son or daughter you can be for your parents.

Furthermore, you have a unique assortment of friends and classmates. You occupy a unique role as an ambassador for Christ where you live and attend school. These are your mission fields, and you are the person God has appointed to serve Him there. Your greatest fulfillment will come from accepting and occupying God's unique place for you to the best of your ability.

Sadly, so many miss their calling in life by looking for fulfillment in the world. Find your fulfillment in the kingdom of God by deciding to be an ambassador for Christ in the world (see 2 Corinthians 5:20).

4. Satisfaction Comes from Living a Quality Life

Satisfaction in life is the result of living righteously and seeking to make everything we're involved in better. Our goal should be to copy Paul's statement of personal satisfaction in what God called him to do: "I have fought the good fight, I have finished the course, I have kept the faith" (2 Timothy 4:7).

Satisfaction comes when we do our best. It is a quality issue, not a quantity issue. You will be more satisfied from doing a few things well than from doing many things in a sloppy or hasty manner. The key to personal satisfaction is not gaining more responsibilities but working hard and doing your best in the responsibilities you have.

The same is true in relationships. If you are unhappy in your relationships, maybe you have spread yourself too thin. Solomon wrote, "A man of many friends comes to ruin, but there is a friend who sticks closer than a brother" (Proverbs 18:24). It may be nice to know a lot of people on the surface, but you need a few real good friends who are committed to a quality relationship with each other.

Our Lord modeled the importance of close relationships. He taught huge groups of people, but He invested most of His time in the 12 disciples. Among those Jesus selected 3—Peter, James and John—to be with Him at some of the most critical times in His ministry. And while suffering on the cross, He committed to John, perhaps His closest friend, the care of His mother. That's a quality relationship, and we all need the satisfaction that quality relationships bring.

5. Happiness Comes from Wanting What You Have

The world's concept of happiness is having what we want. The people on TV tell us we need the latest gadgets and the current trend in clothes or we'll be out of style and have no friends. Thousands of advertised items are better, faster or easier to use than what we already have. We watch the commercials and read the ads, and we go crazy to get all the latest fashions, fads and cool stuff. We're not really happy until we get what we want.

God's concept of happiness is summed up in the words: "Happy is the person who wants what he has." As long as you are focusing on what you don't have, you'll be unhappy. But when you begin to appreciate what you already have, you'll be happy all your life. Satan's lie is that God won't give you what you need or enough of what you need. Paul wrote to Timothy, "Godliness with contentment is great gain. For we brought nothing into the world, and we can take nothing out of it. But if we have food and clothing, we will be content with that" (1 Timothy 6:6-8, *NIV*).

Actually, you already have everything you need to make you happy forever. You have Christ. You have eternal life. You are loved by a heavenly Father who has promised to supply all your needs. No wonder the Bible repeatedly commands us to be thankful (see 1 Thessalonians 5:18). Jesus told us not to worry about what we would eat or drink or wear but to seek His rule in our lives (see Matthew 6:25-34). If you really want to be happy, learn to be thankful for what you have, not greedy for what you don't have.

6. Fun Comes from Enjoying Life Moment by Moment

How much fun are you having as a Christian? Some people think fun is a trip to Disneyland. Yes, there's a lot of fun to be had at Disneyland, but you usually come home with sore feet and used gum stuck to your shoes—and you're out a couple hundred dollars.

Real fun is hanging loose and enjoying life as it happens. Chances are the last time you really had fun it was a spontaneous, spur-of-the-moment activity or event. Big events and expensive outings can be fun, but we tend to plan and spend all the fun right out of them. Sometimes a spontaneous water-balloon fight with friends is as much fun as an expensive concert or trip to Disneyland.

The secret to enjoying life moment by moment as a Christian is in removing the roadblocks. One of the biggest roadblocks to Christian fun is our tendency to keep up appearances. Satan wants us to fear what people say and think about us. We don't want to look out of place or be thought less of by others, so we put on a façade instead of just hanging loose. Fear of what people think moves us to become people-pleasers, and Paul suggested that anybody who lives to please people isn't serving Christ (see Galatians 1:10).

Look at the uninhibited joy in King David, who knew the happiness of being in the presence of the Lord. He was so happy about returning the ark to Jerusalem that he leaped and danced before the Lord in celebration. He knew there was joy in the presence of God. But Michal, his party-pooping wife, thought his behavior was unbecoming for a king, and she told him so. David said, "Forget you, lady. I'm dancing to please the Lord, not you or anybody else. And I'm going to keep dancing whether you like it or not" (a loose paraphrase of 2 Samuel 6:21). As it turned out, Michal was the person God judged in the incident, not David (see 2 Samuel 6:23). You'll find a lot more fun in pleasing the Lord than in trying to please people.

7. Security Comes from Focusing on Eternal Values
The key to experiencing security in our lives is to depend on things that will last for eternity, not just for time. Christians often feel insecure because they are depending on temporal things over which they have no right or ability to control. For example, Rick, a shy, non-athletic guy, wants to hang out with some guys from the football team. Rick is sure the jocks won't accept him on the athletic level. But he has a part-time job and makes good money. So he throws a little of his money around—buying pizza and Cokes for some of the guys. Soon he's accepted as part of the group. His expensive new friendships build his sense of security.

Then one day the boss lays Rick off for a few months. No more pizza parties with the guys. What happens to his security now? It lasts only as long as the money lasts. That's not very solid security.

Security only comes from relating to that which is anchored in eternity. Jesus said that we have eternal life and that no one can snatch us out of His hand (see John 10:27-29). Paul declared that nothing can separate us from the love of God in Christ (see Romans 8:35-39) and that we are sealed in Him by the Holy Spirit (see Ephesians 1:13-14). How much more secure can you get than that?

When we trust in temporal values and relationships, we are always subject to insecurity because these things are subject to failure.

The greatest sense of security you can experience is the byproduct of taking a firm grip on values and relationships that will endure as long as God Himself.

8. Peace Comes from Quieting the Inner Storm

Peace on earth, good will toward men; that's what everybody wants. But nobody can guarantee external peace because nobody can control other people or circumstances. Nations sign and break peace treaties with frightening regularity. One group of peace marchers confronts another group of peace marchers and they end up beating each other over the head with their signs. Kids everywhere say their homes are more like a war zone than a safe haven for family and friends.

The key to experiencing peace is in understanding that it is primarily an internal issue. Peace *with* God is something we already have. As Paul states in Romans 5:1-2, "Therefore, having been justified by faith, we have peace with God through our Lord Jesus Christ, through whom also we have obtained our introduction by faith into this grace in which we stand; and we exult in hope of the glory of God." Peace with God is not something we strive for; it's something we received when we were born again. The rebellion against God is over and our inner world is eternally at peace with God.

The peace *of* God is something we need to take advantage of every day inside us while storms rage in the world around us (see John 14:27). A lot of things can disrupt your external world because you can't control all your circumstances and relationships. For example, if one of your teachers is ticked off at the class and piles on the homework, there's not much you can do about it. But you can control the inner world of your thoughts, emotions and will by allowing the peace of God to rule in your heart on a daily basis. So even though extra homework from an unreasonable teacher ruins your plans for the weekend, it doesn't need to ruin you.

There may be chaos all around you, but God is bigger than any storm. Nothing will happen to you today that God and you can't handle. Your daily time of worship, prayer and reading God's Word will help you get a grip on the peace of God you desire (see Philippians 4:6-7; Colossians 3:15-16).

TRUTH ENCOUNTER

1. Why is it important for you to have the right belief system?
2. Why is it impossible to be living in fear and trust the Lord at the same time?
3. What false beliefs did you spot in your own belief system? How can that change?
4. Write out in your own words a brief description of God's view of success, significance, fulfillment, satisfaction, happiness, fun, security and peace.

Winning the Battle for Your Mind

*"Victory in the battle for our minds is the inheritance
of everyone who is in Christ."*

A few years ago, Shelley attended my (Neil's) class on resolving
spiritual conflicts. At the end of the course she handed me the following letter:

> Dear Neil,
>
> I just want to thank you again for how the Lord has
> used your class to change my life. The last two years of
> my life have been a constant struggle for the control of my
> mind. I was ignorant of my position and authority in Christ,
> and equally ignorant of Satan's ability to deceive me. I was
> constantly afraid. My mind was bombarded by hostile, angry
> thoughts. I felt guilty and wondered what was wrong with
> me. I didn't understand how much bondage I was in until I
> came to your class.
>
> I was always taught that demons didn't really affect
> Christians. But when you began to describe a person influ-
> enced by demons, I just about passed out from shock. You
> were describing me! For the first time in my life I can iden-
> tify Satan's attack and really resist him. I'm not paralyzed
> by fear anymore and my mind is much less cluttered. As
> you can tell, I'm pretty excited about this!
>
> When I read the Scriptures now, I wonder why I
> couldn't see all this before. But as you know, I was deceived.
>
> Thanks again so much.
> Shelley

Shelley struggled in her faith because she didn't understand
the spiritual battle going on for her mind. She was a child of God

all right, but she was a defeated child of God, the unknowing victim of Satan the deceiver. She didn't understand her identity in
Christ or her authority as a believer. She was being "destroyed for
lack of knowledge" (see Hosea 4:6).

Like Shelley, many Christians are spiritually out of touch and
defeated in their daily lives. They don't understand that Satan
is battling to control their minds and ruin their lives. Struggling
believers need a true picture of what is happening in their minds.
They also need to realize that God can renew their minds and free
them from the struggle just as He did for Shelley.

GOD'S WAY VERSUS MAN'S WAY

Faith is God's way to live. Trying to think and reason without God
is man's way to live. God's way and man's way are often in conflict. It's not that living by faith means we disconnect our brains
and ignore our responsibility to think. No, we are required by
God to use our brains and choose the truth. God is a rational God
and He works through our ability to think and reason.

But our ability to direct our lives on our own is limited. The
Lord said, "As the heavens are higher than the earth, so are My ways
higher than your ways, and My thoughts than your thoughts"
(Isaiah 55:9). We don't have the brain power to understand God's
thoughts through human reasoning. That's why we need the Bible,
God's divine revelation.

So we can live God's way by faith, which we will call the "high
road." Or we can live man's way by using our limited ability to understand, which we will call the "low road." The low road describes
our tendency to live independently from God. Solomon urged us
always to live on the high road, God's way, when he wrote, "Do not
lean on your own understanding" (the low road), but "in all your
ways acknowledge Him" (the high road) (Proverbs 3:5-6).

We walk the high road in our lives when we determine to learn
God's plans for us in the Bible and commit ourselves to obey Him.
We walk the low road when we think thoughts and consider plans
that are opposite of what God's Word says. We weaken our commitment to walking the high road whenever we play around with
ideas that are opposite to God's Word.

For example, God's high road for us in school is honesty.
The low road is to cheat. If a Christian studies hard for an impor-

tant exam and prays for God's help, he's walking the high road of faith. But if he decides to take a cheat sheet to class just in case he forgets something, he has made a commitment to the low road. And the more he thinks about low-road options, the more likely he will be to take them.

Don't even consider low-road plans. The more time and energy you spend thinking about your own plans on how to live your life, the less time and energy you have to seek God's plan. The person who flip-flops between God's plan and leaning on his own understanding is called double-minded, "unstable in all his ways" (James 1:8). When you continue to flip-flop, your spiritual growth will slow to a crawl, your maturity in Christ will be blocked and your daily life as a Christian will be marked by discouragement and defeat.

THE SOURCE OF THE LOW ROAD

Where do low-road thoughts come from? There are two main sources.

First, our flesh still sparks low-road thoughts and ideas. The flesh is that part of us that was trained to live independently from God before we became Christians. At that time there was no high road in our lives. We were separated from God, we didn't understand His ways and we learned to succeed and survive by our own abilities. Even though we now have a new nature in Christ, the sinful world still tempts us to return to those old ways of thinking and living.

Second, there is someone active in the world today who hates the high road. Satan and his demons are busy trying to put negative, worldly patterns of thought into our minds that will bring out negative, worldly patterns of behavior.

The battle for our minds is a conflict between the high road, living God's way by faith, and the low road, living man's way by following the desires of the world, the flesh and the devil. You may feel like you are the helpless victim in this battle, being slapped back and forth like a hockey puck. But you are anything but helpless. In fact, you are the one who determines the winner in every battle between the high road and the low road.

STRONGHOLDS ARE THE PRIME TARGET OF OUR WARFARE

The battle for the mind is explained in 2 Corinthians 10:3-5:

> For though we live in the world, we do not wage war as the world does. The weapons we fight with are not the weapons of the world. On the contrary, they have divine power to demolish strongholds. We demolish arguments and every pretension that sets itself up against the knowledge of God, and we take captive every thought to make it obedient to Christ (*NIV*).

The first thing we need to know about the battle for our minds is that it is not fought on the level of human ability. We can't outsmart or outmuscle the flesh or the devil on our own. Our weapons must have "divine power" if we are going to win a spiritual conflict.

The main targets that must be destroyed are the "strongholds" in the mind. Strongholds are bad patterns of thought that are burned into our minds either through repetition over time or through one-time, deeply shocking experiences. How are these strongholds established in our minds? Usually they are the result of a number of subtle steps that lead us away from God's plan for us and trap us in low-road behavior.

Our Environment

Remember Mr. Rogers and his beautiful neighborhood? Every day was wonderful, and there were no problems that a couple of hand puppets and the man with the sweater and sneakers couldn't solve. It was an ideal world. The real world is quite different.

We were designed to live in fellowship with God and fulfill His purposes. But we were born physically alive and spiritually dead in a world opposed to God's design (see Ephesians 2:1-2). Before we came to Christ, all our experiences came from this sinful environment. Every day we lived in this environment we were influenced and shaped by it.

The worldly influences we have been exposed to include people, places and events that have tempted us to travel the low road. We have also been influenced by books we read, movies we watched, music we listened to and even shocking events such as a car accident or a death in the family. We learned ways (which may or may not have been God's way) to cope with what happened to us and to solve the problems they produced. If you grew up in a non-Christian home, you learned how to survive, cope and succeed in this world apart from God.

When you became a Christian, your sins were washed away, but your old ways of thinking and behaving, which you learned as you adjusted to your environment, remained. In fact, a born-again believer can continue to live out the same basic lifestyle she had while she was living independently of God. That is why Paul writes that we are not to be conformed to this world but transformed by the renewing of our minds (see Romans 12:2).

Temptation

Whenever we feel attracted to the low-road plan instead of God's high-road plan for our lives, we are experiencing temptation. The purpose of all temptation is to get us to take the low road, to fill genuine needs through the world, the flesh and the devil instead of in Christ. That's the great contest. And Satan knows just which buttons to push to tempt us away from depending on Christ. He has watched your behavior over the years and he knows where you are weak, and that's where he attacks.

Consideration and Choice

The moment we are tempted to get a need met in the world instead of in Christ, we are on the threshold of a decision. If we don't immediately choose to "take captive every thought to make it obedient to Christ" (2 Corinthians 10:5, NIV), we will begin to consider it as an option. And if we begin to think about it, immediately our emotions will be affected and the likelihood of yielding to that temptation is increased.

A humorous "Cathy" cartoon strip shows the serious consequences of considering a tempting thought instead of immediately dismissing it. Cathy is struggling with her diet. Notice how her unchecked thoughts carry her away like a runaway freight train:

Frame 1:   I will take a drive, but won't go near the grocery store.

Frame 2:   I will drive by the grocery store, but will not go in.

Frame 3:   I will go into the grocery store, but will not
             walk down the aisle where the Halloween
             candy is on sale.
Frame 4:   I will look at the candy, but not pick it up.
Frame 5:   I will pick it up, but not buy it.
Frame 6:   I will buy it, but not open it.
Frame 7:   Open it, but not smell it.
Frame 8:   Smell it, but not taste it.
Frame 9:   Taste it, but not eat it.
Frame 10:   *Eat, eat, eat, eat, eat!*

The Bible teaches us that God has provided a way of escape from every temptation (see 1 Corinthians 10:13). But the escape is at the threshold. If you don't control the temptation when the thought first occurs, you run the risk of allowing the temptation to control you.

For example, a guy sees a pornographic magazine and is tempted toward lust. He could say, "My relationship with sin is over. I don't have to give in to this. I choose right now not to look at it and not to think about it." Then he separates himself from the picture immediately and escapes the lust.

But if he hesitates, stares at the picture and begins to fantasize about it, he will trigger an emotional landslide and a physical response that will be difficult to stop. He must capture the tempting thought at the threshold or it will probably capture him.

Action, Habit and Stronghold

People who study human behavior tell us that if we continue to repeat an act for six weeks, it will become a habit. And if we exercise that habit long enough, a stronghold will be established. A stronghold is a low-road pattern of thinking that is deeply burned into our minds. Once a stronghold of thought and response has formed a groove in our minds, choosing and acting contrary to that pattern is very difficult.

Hostility is a stronghold. God's Word tells us to love and pray for our enemies. If you can't help fighting with those who oppose you, you may have learned to cope that way and your low-road response has become a stronghold.

Inferiority is a stronghold. As a Christian, you are a child of God, a saint who is inferior to no one. If you are constantly shrinking back from people because of feelings of inferiority, it's because the world, the flesh and the devil have carved a negative, low-road groove in your mind over the years.

Manipulation is a stronghold. Do you feel like you must control the people and circumstances in your life? Is it nearly impossible for you to give a problem to God and not worry about it? Somewhere in your past you may have developed a pattern of control that now masters you. It's a stronghold.

Sexual addiction is a stronghold. If you can't keep yourself from thinking about or looking at the opposite sex without impure thoughts and desires, a stronghold of lust may have taken root in your mind.

Homosexuality is a stronghold. In God's eyes there is no such thing as a homosexual. He created us male and female. But there is homosexual behavior, which can usually be traced to past negative experiences with parents or sex. Such experiences prompted these individuals to doubt their sexual adequacy and they began to believe a lie about their sexual identity.

Eating disorders like anorexia or bulimia are strongholds. Here is an 89-pound girl standing in front of a mirror believing that she is fat. Have you ever seen a lie more obvious than that? She is the victim of negative thought patterns about herself that have been burned into her mind and direct all her activities concerning her body and the proper use of food.

Any knee-jerk response that directs your thinking and acting in a negative, low-road manner is a stronghold in the mind. Any wrong behavior you can't control may spring from a stronghold. Somewhere in the past you knowingly or unknowingly formed a pattern of thinking and behaving that now controls you.

IN ORDER TO WIN THE BATTLE FOR YOUR MIND, YOU NEED A PLAN

Must these negative patterns of behavior control you? Absolutely not! Anything that has been learned can be unlearned. If your mind has been programmed wrong, it can be reprogrammed. By hearing God's Word being taught, studying your Bible and living as Christ's disciple, you can stop being conformed to this world and experience the transformation of the renewing of your mind (see Romans 12:2).

If your past experiences were spiritually or emotionally devastating, Christ-centered counseling will help you resolve the conflicts. Since some of these strongholds are thoughts raised up against the knowledge of God (see 2 Corinthians 10:5), learning to know God as a loving Father and yourself as His accepted child is your starting place.

But there's more going on in our minds than the bad patterns we have developed. We're also up against the devil, who is scheming to fill our mind with thoughts that are opposed to God's plan for us. We must capture the enemy's thoughts and make them obey Christ before they prompt us to take the low road (see 2 Corinthians 10:5).

Satan's plan is to put his thoughts and ideas into our minds and deceive us into believing that they are ours. It happened to King David. Satan "moved David to number Israel" (1 Chronicles 21:1), an act God had forbidden, and David acted on Satan's idea. Did Satan walk up to David one day and say, "I want you to number Israel"? I doubt it. David was a godly man and he wouldn't have obeyed Satan. But what if Satan slipped the idea into David's mind this way: "I need to know how large my army is; I think I'll count the troops"?

If Satan can place a thought in our minds—and he can—it isn't much more of a trick for him to make us think it's our idea. If we knew it was Satan, we'd reject the thought, right? But when he disguises his suggestion as our idea, we are more likely to accept it and act on it.

In Acts 5 we read about Ananias and Sapphira being struck dead for lying. They may have thought it was their idea to hold back some of their offering while getting the strokes and attention from others who believed they had given everything. If they knew that it was Satan's idea, they probably wouldn't have done it. But the Bible clearly says that Satan filled their heart to lie to the Holy Spirit (see Acts 5:1-3).

If Satan can get us to believe a lie, he can control our lives.

EXPOSE THE LIE AND YOU WIN THE BATTLE

Satan's power is in the lie. Jesus said, "The devil . . . does not stand in the truth, because there is no truth in him. Whenever he speaks a lie, he speaks from his own nature; for he is a liar, and the father of lies" (John 8:44). Satan has no power over us except what we give him. When we fail to take every thought captive, we can be deceived into believing his lies.

Satan can introduce his thoughts into our minds like silent inner voices. Many Christians we talk to clearly hear voices in their mind, but they are afraid to tell anyone for fear that others will think they have a mental problem. More than 1,200 Christian high school students were asked, "Have you heard 'voices' in your head like there was a subconscious self talking to you, or have you struggled with really bad thoughts?" Seventy percent answered yes!

Many Christians are plagued with bad thoughts that stop or hinder their personal devotions. Seldom do they realize that these distractions reflect the battle going on for their minds, even though Paul warned us, "The Spirit explicitly says that in latter times some will fall away from the faith, paying attention to deceitful spirits and doctrines of demons" (1 Timothy 4:1).

Since Satan's primary weapon is the lie, our defense against him is the truth. When you expose Satan's lie with God's truth, his power is broken. That's why Jesus said, "You shall know the truth, and the truth shall make you free" (John 8:32). That's why He prayed, "My prayer is . . . that you protect them from the evil one. . . . Sanctify them by the truth; your word is truth" (John 17:15,17, *NIV*). That's why the first piece of armor Paul mentions for standing against the schemes of the devil is the belt of truth (see Ephesians 6:14). Satan's lie cannot withstand the truth any more than the darkness of night can withstand the light of the rising sun.

What is our part in the battle? First, we must be transformed by the renewing of our minds (see Romans 12:2). How do you renew your mind? By filling it with God's Word. In order to win the battle for your mind, you must "let the peace of Christ rule in your hearts" (Colossians 3:15) and let "the word of Christ richly dwell within you" (Colossians 5:16). As you continue to fill your mind with God's truth, you will equip yourself to recognize the lie and take it captive.

Second, Peter told us to prepare our minds for action (see 1 Peter 1:13). Do away with fruitless fantasy. To imagine yourself doing things without ever doing anything is dangerous. You will lose touch with reality. But if you imagine yourself traveling the high road by obeying the truth, you can move yourself toward living that way. For example, if you read about caring for the poor in your devotions, you can prepare your mind for action by planning ways to use some of your own money to help the homeless. Just be sure you follow through by doing what you imagine.

Third, take every thought captive and make it obedient to Christ (see 2 Corinthians 10:5). When a thought pops into your mind that doesn't agree with God's Word, refuse it right away. Choose instead to believe and act on the truth.

Fourth, turn to God. When your commitment to the high road is being challenged by low-road thoughts from the world, the flesh or the devil, bring it to God in prayer (see Philippians 4:6). By doing so you are acknowledging God and exposing your thoughts to His truth. Your double-mindedness will dissolve "and the peace of God . . . shall guard your hearts and your minds in Christ Jesus" (Philippians 4:7).

As we turn to God, He will do His part. But we must assume responsibility for our own thoughts as directed by Philippians 4:8-9:

> Whatever is true, whatever is honorable, whatever is right, whatever is pure, whatever is lovely, whatever is of good repute, if there is any excellence and if anything worthy of praise, let your mind dwell on these things. The things you have learned and received and heard and seen in me, practice these things; and the God of peace shall be with you.

Victory in the battle for our minds is the inheritance of everyone who is in Christ.

TRUTH ENCOUNTER

1. Why is the low road still present and often attractive to us as believers? How can we avoid it?
2. Why can't the battle for the mind be fought just on a human level?
3. What are some strongholds in your life?
4. How do you break down a stronghold?

You must be real in order to be right

"Perhaps our prayers at times of hurt or trouble are not the best. But they are real and honest before God."

The following story illustrates how our feelings are directed by what we believe.

Ten-year-old Matthew is a great kid. He's fun to be around, and he usually has a positive attitude. Matthew also has excellent athletic abilities. He loves to play baseball and has been in Little League since he was six years old.

But last year, whenever Matthew struck out he really got down on himself. By the end of the season he began to act out his negative feelings by checking out of the game mentally. No amount of encouragement would cheer him up. At the same time he became fearful of being left home alone and especially of sleeping alone in his room. He slipped into a depression that frightened his parents. He seemed distant and detached from reality. Just putting Matthew to bed was an agonizing experience. His parents had to spend an inordinate amount of time assuring him that the house was secure and that he was safe.

Three weeks into Matthew's depression, his parents attended one of my (Neil's) classes on resolving spiritual conflicts. By the end of the class, they knew that Matthew was under demonic attack. The father explained in a letter:

> Neil,
>
> I took Matthew out for a walk Friday evening after the class was over and asked him if he felt hopeless. He said yes. He also said he was scared but didn't know why. I held him and we prayed for several minutes. I shared with him about his identity in Christ and his secure relationship with his Heavenly Father. I told him about his authority in Christ to stand against the enemy . . . He was all ears!

I shared with him how he could stand against Satan at home in his room. From that moment Matthew was a different boy. His whole countenance changed. The depression lifted immediately. His fear at night gradually disappeared. . . . I believe Matthew now knows what it means to be a child of God. No longer is his identity wrapped up in his performance. He really seems to be free, and it is incredible to watch him grow in his relationship with the Lord.[1]

Matthew had some wrong beliefs. He believed that his self-worth was dependent upon how well he played baseball. What a lie! Satan also convinced him to stuff his feelings inside so that he wouldn't discover that they were based on lies.

Satan's plan failed with Matthew. When his dad took him for a walk, Matthew opened up and his dad was able to help him understand his true identity and worth as a child of God. As soon as Matthew discovered his false beliefs and got rid of them, his depression lifted.

OUR EMOTIONS REVEAL WHAT WE'RE THINKING

Our emotions play a big role in the process of renewing our minds. In a general sense, our emotions are a product of our thought life. If we don't think right—meaning we're not seeing God and His Word properly—we won't feel right.

One of the best scriptural illustrations of the relationship between beliefs and emotions is found in Lamentations 3.

Jeremiah was really bummed out when he wrongly thought that God was against him and that He was the cause of his physical problems:

I am the man who has seen affliction because of the rod of His wrath. He has driven me and made me walk in darkness and not in light. Surely against me He has turned His hand repeatedly all the day. He has caused my flesh and my skin to waste away, He has broken my bones. He has besieged and encompassed me with bitterness and hardship. In dark places He has made me dwell, like those who have long been dead (Lamentations 3:1-6).

Jeremiah also felt trapped and afraid:

> He has walled me in so that I cannot go out; He has made my chain heavy. Even when I cry out and call for help, He shuts out my prayer. He has blocked my ways with hewn stone; He has made my paths crooked. He is to me like a bear lying in wait, like a lion in secret places. He has turned aside my ways and torn me to pieces; He has made me desolate. . . . So I say, "My strength has perished, and so has my hope from the Lord" (Lamentations 3:7-11,18).

What was Jeremiah's problem? His beliefs about God were way off center because of the pain of suffering. God wasn't the cause of his problems. But Jeremiah wasn't thinking right, believing right or seeing his circumstances right, so he wasn't feeling right or responding right either.

But then Jeremiah began to sing a different tune:

> Remember my affliction and my wandering, the wormwood and the bitterness. Surely my soul remembers and is bowed down within me. This I recall to my mind, therefore I have hope. The Lord's lovingkindnesses indeed never cease, for His compassions never fail. They are new every morning; great is Thy faithfulness. "The Lord is my portion," says my soul, "therefore I have hope in Him" (Lamentations 3:19-24).

What a turn around! Did God change? Did Jeremiah's circumstances change? No. His beliefs about God changed, and when they did his emotions also changed. Jeremiah was honest with God about his pain and his feelings. He did not stuff his hurt inside. He told God how he felt and his honesty helped him turn wrong thinking into right thinking.

WHAT YOU SEE IS WHAT YOU THINK

We are not shaped as much by what's happening around us as we are by how we view what's happening around us. Life's events don't control who we are; God determines who we are, and our view of life's events determines how well we will handle the pressures of life.

We are tempted to say, "He made me so mad!" or "I wasn't depressed until she showed up!" That's like saying, "I have no control over my emotions or my will." In reality we have very little control over our feelings, but we do have control over our thoughts, and our thoughts determine our feelings and how we act. That's why it is so important that we fill our mind with the knowledge of God and His Word. We need to see life from God's point of view and respond accordingly.

If what we believe isn't based on God's truth, then what we feel won't reflect reality. Telling someone that they shouldn't feel a certain way about something doesn't help. They can do little about how they feel. The real problem is that they have some wrong beliefs about God or their problem. Those wrong beliefs are making them feel the way they do.

For example, suppose your dream of owning your own car was in the hands of your mom and dad. You and all your friends are praying like crazy that they will let you buy a car. But you get home one evening and happen to hear your mom and dad talking in the other room. Your heart sinks as you hear them say there is no way they are going to let you buy a car. Where would your feelings go in a matter of seconds? To the bottom!

But you only heard half the truth! What you didn't hear was that your parents decided to buy the car for you. What you first believed didn't reflect truth, so what you felt didn't reflect reality.

Imagine that a friend, who knows about your parents' plan to buy you a car, comes over to congratulate you before you know the whole story. He expects to find you overjoyed, but instead you're in the pits. So he says, "Congratulations on the car."

"Congratulations?" you say. "What are you, a sick-o?"

"Why are you feeling that way? You should be happy that your parents are buying a car for you."

What happens to your feelings now that you know the whole truth? You hit the ceiling with joy. Our feelings always react to what we think is true and choose to believe, whether it's the truth or not.

The order of Scripture is to know the truth, believe it, walk according to it and let our emotions be a result of our obedience. When you believe what you feel instead of the truth, how will your walk be? As inconsistent as your feelings. But when you believe and act on the truth, your feelings will reflect reality. Jesus said, "If you know these things, you are blessed if you do them" (John 13:17). Knowing and doing comes first.

Our emotions are more than just a tailgate, however. They play an important role in our day-to-day life.

DON'T IGNORE THE WARNING SIGNS OF YOUR EMOTIONS

I (Neil) played sports as a young man and I have the scars on my knees to prove it. The incision of my first knee surgery cut across a nerve and I had no feeling around that area of my leg for several months. Sometimes I would sit down to watch TV and, without thinking, rest a cup of hot coffee on my numb knee. I couldn't feel anything, but before long I could sure smell something: my skin burning! For a while I had a neat little brown ring on the top of my knee, the result of not being able to feel.

Our emotions are to our soul what our physical feelings are to our body. Nobody in his or her right mind enjoys pain. But if you didn't feel pain, you would be in danger of serious injury and infection. And if you didn't feel anger, sorrow or joy, your soul would be in trouble. Emotions are God's emergency warning system to let you know what is going on inside. Feelings are neither good nor bad. They're just part of being human. Just like you respond to the warnings of physical pain, so you need to learn to respond to your emotional warning signals.

We have three options for responding to our emotions. First, we can stuff them inside and try to ignore them. Second, we can let them all hang out, thoughtlessly lashing out or flying off the handle. Third, we can honestly acknowledge our feelings to God and ourselves.

Stuffing Our Emotions
Those who stuff their emotions inside ignore their feelings and choose not to deal with them. King David had something to say about the ugly impact of stuffing his feelings and failing to acknowledge his sin with God: "When I kept silent, my bones wasted away through my groaning all day long. . . . Let everyone who is godly pray to you while you may be found; surely when the mighty waters rise, they will not reach him" (Psalm 32:3,6, *NIV*).

When you are hurt or in trouble, your problems seem bigger than God. If you believe that, it won't take long for your emotions to overcome you. When your feelings build up around you like "mighty waters," you won't turn to God. Your emotions will be in control. It's important to open up to God while you can, because if you bottle up your feelings too long, it can short-circuit your relationship with Him.

Letting It All Hang Out

Another unhealthy way to respond to emotions is to thoughtlessly let them all hang out, telling anybody and everybody exactly how we feel. We have all seen kids and adults who lose control of their emotions and explode with hurtful words or actions.

The apostle Peter is a great example in this area. Peter had no problem telling anyone what was on his mind or how he felt. But his unbridled expression of his emotions got him into trouble more than once. One minute Peter makes the greatest confession of all time: "You [Jesus] are the Christ, the Son of the living God" (Matthew 16:16, NIV). But a few minutes later he tells Jesus He doesn't know what He's doing, and Jesus has to rebuke him: "Get behind Me, Satan!" (Matthew 16:22-23).

It was Peter who promised to follow Jesus anywhere, even to the death. But then, only hours later, Peter swore that he never knew Him. The fact that Peter later became a leader of the New Testament Church shows the powerful change that the Holy Spirit can produce.

Letting your emotions all hang out may be somewhat healthy for you, but it is usually unhealthy for others around you. "There, I'm glad I got that off my chest," you say after an outburst. But in the process you just destroyed your friend or family member. James warned, "Let every one be quick to hear, slow to speak and slow to anger; for the anger of man does not achieve the righteousness of God" (James 1:19-20). Paul urged, "Be angry, and yet do not sin" (Ephesians 4:26). If you wish to be angry and not sin, then be angry the way Christ was: be angry at sin. Jesus turned over the tables in the Temple, not the people who were doing business there.

Acknowledging Our Emotions

Nancy was a college student in another city who drove to Los Angeles to talk to me (Neil) about her difficult relationship with her mother. But we ended up talking more about Nancy's inability to express the anger and resentment she felt in the relationship. "My roommate gets to the point sometimes where she just explodes emotionally to let off steam. I have deep feelings too, but I'm not sure that a Christian is supposed to let off steam."

I opened my Bible to Psalm 109 and read David's prayer about his enemy, including the words:

> Let his days be few. . . . Let his children be fatherless, and his wife a widow. Let his children wander about and beg; and let them seek sustenance far from their ruined homes. Let the creditor seize all that he has; and let strangers plunder the product of his labor. Let there be none to extend lovingkindness to him, nor any to be gracious to his fatherless children. Let his posterity be cut off; in a following generation let their name be blotted out (Psalm 109:8-13).

"What's that doing in the Bible?" Nancy gasped. "How could David pray all those evil things about his enemy? How could he talk to God that way? That's pure hatred."

"David's words didn't surprise God," I answered. "God already knew how he thought and felt. David was simply expressing his pain and anger honestly to God who understood how he felt and accepted him where he was."

After a couple of thoughtful moments, Nancy asked, "Does that mean it's okay to do what I do?"

"What do you do?"

"Well," she said, looking slightly embarrassed, "when the pressure builds up inside, I go off by myself and scream and holler and shout and kick. When I get back to the dorm I feel better."

I encouraged Nancy that when she is able to dump her hurt and hatred before God, she probably won't dump it on her roommate or her mother in a destructive way. I also reminded her that David was as honest about his need for God as he was about expressing his feelings. He closed the psalm by praying, "Help me, O Lord my God. . . . With my mouth, I will give thanks abundantly to the Lord" (Psalm 109:26,30).

The way David and Nancy acknowledged their feelings is healthy. Perhaps our prayers at times of hurt or trouble are not the best. But they are real and honest before God. If we come to our prayer time feeling angry, depressed or frustrated, and then pretend to be happy and joyful, as if God doesn't know how we feel, is He pleased? Not at all. In God's eyes, if we're not real, we're not right.

Getting in touch with our emotions also involves being real in front of a few trusted friends. We shouldn't let off steam just anywhere in front of just anybody. That's letting it all hang out and we run the risk of hurting others more than we help ourselves—and that's wrong. The biblical pattern seems to suggest that you have a few intimate friends you can share deeply with. During his travels, Paul had Barnabas, Silas or Timothy to lean on. In the Garden of Gethsemane, Jesus expressed His grief to His inner circle of Peter, James and John.

It is difficult for a person to maintain mental health unless he has at least one person with whom he can be emotionally honest. If you have two or three people like this in your life, you are truly blessed.

EMOTIONAL HONESTY: HOW TO DISH IT OUT AND HOW TO TAKE IT

As a young pastor I (Neil) received one of those middle-of-the-night telephone calls that every pastor dreads: "Pastor, our son has been in an accident. They don't expect him to live. Could you please come to the hospital?"

I arrived at the hospital about one in the morning. I sat with the parents in the waiting room, hoping and praying for the best but fearing the worst. About 4:00 A.M. the doctor came out to give us the worst: "We lost him."

Naturally, the family was devastated. But I was so tired and emotionally drained that instead of offering words of comfort, I just sat there and cried with them. I couldn't think of anything to say. I went home feeling that I had failed the family in their darkest hour.

Soon after the accident the young man's parents moved away. But about five years later they stopped by the church for a visit and took me out to lunch. "Neil, we'll never forget what you did for us when our son died," they said.

"What did I do?" I asked, still feeling that I had failed them. "I felt your pain but I didn't know what to say."

"We didn't need words; we needed love. We knew you loved us because you cried with us."

One of our challenges in the area of emotions is in learning how to respond to others when they honestly tell us their feelings. Words aren't the important issue when someone is experiencing great inner pain. We shouldn't respond to their words; we should respond to their pain. The harshness of their words only indicates how bad they are hurting. When grief-stricken Mary and Martha greeted Jesus with the news of Lazarus's death, He didn't preach to them; He wept (see John 11:35). Paul commanded, "Rejoice with those who rejoice, and weep with those who weep" (Romans 12:15).

Even though words are not the most important thing in acknowledging emotions, we can guard our relationships by expressing how we feel with kindness. Proverbs 15:1 says, "A gentle answer turns away wrath, but a harsh word stirs up anger" (*NIV*).

For example, you're having a terrible day at school, so you call home and say to your mom, "I have to stay after school and won't be home until about 6:00 P.M. Could you wash my football uniform for tonight's game?" And she says she will.

When you hit the front door, you are physically and emotionally wiped out. Then you discover that your mom doesn't have your uniform ready. "What's the deal?" you blaze at her. "I need my uniform for tonight's game. There's no way it's going to be ready in time!" Then you slam the door and storm off.

Is your mom really the cause of your emotional outburst? Not really. She just triggered the explosion. The dynamite was already in place. You had a terrible day and you're tired, hungry and bummed out. It's not her fault. Anything could have set you off. You could have just as easily kicked the dog. Yet you level your mom and chalk it up to emotional honesty.

Don't abandon love in your willingness to be honest. Upon learning that your football uniform is not ready, you could say, "Mom, I'm feeling wiped out." That kind of non-attacking honesty accomplishes two important things. First, by not blaming your mom, you let her off the hook. She knows you're not mad at her. Second, since she doesn't have to defend herself, she is free to meet your needs. She can say, "I'll have the uniform ready in a few minutes."

When it comes to acknowledging emotions with your family and friends, honesty is the best policy. But be sure to speak the truth in love (see Ephesians 4:15).

Another important guideline for your emotions is to know your limits. Be aware that if you're seriously angry, tense, anxious or depressed, it's not a good time to make decisions on important issues. You may say or do something you'll later regret. Somebody's going to get hurt. You're far better off to know your emotional limits and say, "If we keep talking, I'm going to get angry. Can we talk about this a little later?"

Realize also that there are a lot of physical factors that will affect your emotional limits. As a teenager, your body is changing so fast that some days you feel like you're going to explode. Growing from boy to man or girl to woman is a huge change. Understand that during this time of your life, you're more emotionally charged than normal. Be careful not to let your emotions get out of control.

If you're hungry, postpone a potentially explosive conversation until after you eat. If you're tired, get a good night's sleep. Girls, be aware that during your menstrual cycle there will be days that will be more difficult than others emotionally. And guys, you will be wise to understand that your mom, sisters and female friends have shorter emotional fuses during these times. Try to be sensitive to their emotional needs. Their attitude is being affected by what they are experiencing physically.

The important process of renewing your mind includes acknowledging your emotions honestly and expressing them lovingly. Dealing with your emotions properly is an important step in keeping the devil from gaining a place in your life.

TRUTH ENCOUNTER

1. What do think your emotions reveal about you?
2. In what ways is stuffing your emotions dangerous or hurtful to you? What are some alternatives to stuffing your emotions?
3. "It's not very Christlike to tell God you're angry or that you're experiencing hatred." Do you agree or disagree with this statement? Why?
4. In what ways can just "blowing up" hurt people?

Note
1. Neil T. Anderson and Steve Russo, *The Seduction of Our Children* (Eugene, OR: Harvest House Publishers, 1991), pp. 107-108. Used by permission.

HEALING EMOTIONAL WOUNDS FROM YOUR PAST

"We must learn how to resolve past problems or our hurt will keep building up as we continue to withdraw from life."

Dan and Cindy were a fine young Christian couple who were preparing for ministry on the mission field. Then tragedy struck. Cindy was raped, and the event tore the couple up inside. The shock was so severe that they moved to another town. As hard as she tried to get back to normal life, Cindy couldn't shake the horrible memories and feelings from her experience.

Six months after the rape, Dan and Cindy attended a church conference where I (Neil) was speaking. During the conference, Cindy called me in tears. "Neil, I just can't get over this thing. I know God can turn everything into good, but how is He going to do that? Every time I think about what happened I start to cry."

"Wait a minute, Cindy," I said. "You've misunderstood something. God will work everything out for good, but He doesn't make a bad thing good. What happened to you was very bad. God's good thing is to show you how you can walk through your crisis and come out of it a better person."

"But I just can't separate myself from my experience," she sobbed. "I've been raped, Neil, and I'll be a victim of that all my life."

"No, Cindy," I insisted. "The rape happened to you, but it hasn't changed who you are, nor does it have to control you. You were the victim of a terrible, ugly tragedy. But if you only see yourself as a rape victim for the rest of your life, you will never get over your tragedy. You're a child of God. No event or person, good or bad, can rob you of that."

Cindy got a grip on the truth that Jesus Christ, not her past hurts, determines her identity. She and Dan are serving the Lord today.

BAD THINGS DO HAPPEN TO GOOD PEOPLE

All of us have a number of hurtful, upsetting experiences in our past that have scarred us emotionally. You may have been physically, emotionally or sexually abused by a family member. You may have been severely frightened as a child. You may have suffered through a painful relationship: a broken friendship, the sudden death of someone special to you, the divorce of your parents. One or more shocking, hurtful events may have caused deep inner pain that has hindered your growth as a Christian.

Unlike our day-to-day emotions that vary according to how we think, the pain from past hurts is always there. Certain topics can trigger these hurts and cause a strong emotional reaction. For example, you may have felt something when you read Cindy's story at the start of this chapter. If you or a close friend have been raped, just the mention of rape may have sparked anger, hatred or fear in you. However, if you have only read about rape victims but never been one or known one, your emotional response may have been very low.

Even something as simple as a name can prompt an emotional reaction. If your kind, loving grandfather is (or was) named Bill, you probably have a good feeling toward other men named Bill. But if as a child you had a neighbor named Bill who frightened you or abused you, you may not feel so good about other men you meet named Bill.

Let's call these long-term feelings, which hide deep inside us, *primary emotions*. The power of our primary emotions is determined by our past experiences. The more shocking and painful the experience was, the stronger will be our primary emotion.

Many of our primary emotions lie hidden within us and have very little effect on our lives until something comes along to trigger them. Have you ever brought up a topic of conversation that upset someone and sent him storming out of the room? *What set him off?* you wondered. He was set off by a bad experience in his past that was triggered by your topic. The trigger can be anything in the present that links a person with his past conflict.

Most people try to control their primary emotions by avoiding the people or events that trigger them. But we can't cut ourselves off completely from everything that may set off negative feelings. We are bound to see something on TV or hear something in a conversation that will bring to mind an unpleasant experience. We must learn how to resolve past problems or our hurt will keep building up as we continue to withdraw from life.

LEARNING TO RESOLVE PRIMARY EMOTIONS

We have no control over a primary emotion when it is triggered. It doesn't do any good to feel guilty about something we have no control over. But we can take a close look at the situation to bring it under control.

For example, suppose you meet a man named Bill. He looks a little like the Bill who abused you as a child. Even though he's not the same person, you have strong feelings of fear or dislike for him. But you quickly remind yourself that this is not the same Bill. And when you begin to think properly about Bill, your negative emotion will be transformed into a more positive one. This is how we get a grip on reality when negative emotions from past experiences try to rule our daily lives.

You have used this process lots of times and also helped others do it. Someone gets ticked off, so you get in his face and tell him to cool down and get real. You are helping that person gain control of himself by making him think. Notice how this works the next time you watch a football game and tempers explode on the field. One player grabs an angry teammate and says, "Listen, Meathead, you're going to cost us a 15-yard penalty and perhaps the game if you don't simmer down." Later the player will see the conflict in perspective and even feel a little silly about it.

Most people we counsel have had serious hurts in the past. Some have experienced such abuse that they have no conscious memory of their experiences. Others avoid any people or experiences that will bring back those bad memories. Some who remember but don't want to deal with it act like it never happened. Others try to cover over the pain with food, drugs or sex.

This is not God's way. God does everything in the light. He knows best when to bring past problems into the light to be dealt with. God also allows each person to grow in his Christian life to the point where he is able to face the past. And if God doesn't reveal a painful memory, there's a good reason for it. We have prayed with many people that God would reveal anything in the past that is keeping them in bondage to their pain—and God has answered those prayers in His time.

Psalm 139:23-24 reads, "Search me, O God, and know my heart; try me and know my anxious thoughts; and see if there be any hurtful way in me, and lead me in the everlasting way." God knows about the hidden hurts within you that you may not be able to see. When you ask God to search your heart, He will show you those dark areas of your past and bring them to light at the right time.

SEE YOUR PAST IN THE LIGHT OF WHO YOU ARE

So, how does God want us to resolve these past experiences? In two ways. First, we have the privilege of looking at them in the light of who we are now as opposed to who we were then. Refuse to believe that you are a slave to your past experiences. As a Christian, you are the product of the work of Christ on the cross. You are literally a new creature in Christ (see 2 Corinthians 5:17). Old things, including the shocking pain of past experiences, are passed away. The old you is gone; the new you is here. The way you handled those experiences without Christ may still be programmed in your memory, but you are now free to respond in a new way in Christ.

People who have been hurt in the past have their emotions stuck up near the ceiling. When a present event sparks that primary emotion, they believe what they feel instead of believing what is true. For example, people who have been verbally abused by their parents have a hard time believing they are completely loved by Father God. Their primary emotions argue that they are unloved by their parent. If they have been told all their lives that they will never amount to anything, they find it hard to believe that they are loved and valued by God. They believe what they feel and their walk is off course.

Now that you are in Christ, you can look at those events from the perspective of who you are today. You may be struggling with the question, "Where was God when all this was going on?" He was there as others hurt you or as you made some bad choices. But don't worry about what was going on then. The truth is, He is in your life right now desiring to set you free from your past. You can't fix your past, but you can be free from it. Seeing past events through your new identity in Christ is what starts the process of healing those damaged emotions.

FORGIVE THOSE WHO HAVE HURT YOU IN THE PAST

The second step in resolving past problems is to forgive those who have hurt you. After encouraging Cindy to see her rape in light of who she is in Christ, I (Neil) said, "Cindy, you also need to forgive the man who raped you." Cindy's response was typical of many believers who have suffered physical, sexual or emotional pain at the hands of others: "How can I forgive him? What he did was wrong."

Perhaps you have asked the same question. Why should you forgive those who have hurt you in the past?

First, forgiveness is required by God. As soon as Jesus spoke the amen to His model prayer—which included a request for God's forgiveness—He commented, "If you forgive men for their transgressions, your heavenly Father will also forgive you. But if you do not forgive men, then your Father will not forgive your transgressions" (Matthew 6:14-15). We must base our relationships with others on the same standard on which God bases His relationship with us: love, acceptance and forgiveness (see Matthew 18:21-35).

Second, forgiveness is necessary to avoid being trapped by Satan. Unforgiveness is a primary means Satan uses to gain entrance to believers' lives. Paul encouraged people to forgive each other "in order that no advantage be taken of us by Satan; for we are not ignorant of his schemes" (2 Corinthians 2:11). Unforgiveness is an open invitation to Satan's bondage in our lives.

Third, forgiveness is to be the normal way of life for all Christians. Paul wrote, "Let all bitterness and wrath and anger and clamor and slander be put away from you, along with all malice. And be kind to one another, tender-hearted, forgiving each other, just as God in Christ also has forgiven you" (Ephesians 4:31-32).

What Is Forgiveness?

In order to understand what forgiveness *is*, we must first see what it is *not*.

Forgiveness is not forgetting. People who try to forgive by forgetting hurts they have suffered usually fail to do both. The Bible says that God will not remember our sins (see Hebrews 10:17). But God knows everything, so He can't forget. What it means is that God will not bring up our past sins and use them against us (see Psalm 103:12). It is possible to forgive without forgetting.

Forgiveness does not mean that you must put up with someone's sin. Beth, a college girl, came to me (Dave) in tears, explaining that her mother continued to abuse her verbally and control her as she had during childhood. Beth had no desire to forgive her mother since she fully expected to be hurt again and again. "Am I supposed to let her keep ruining my life?" Beth demanded.

No, forgiving someone doesn't mean that you must be a doormat to his or her continual sin. I encouraged Beth to lovingly but firmly tell her mother that she would no longer tolerate verbal abuse and manipulation. It's okay to forgive another's past sins and, at the same time, take a stand against future sins. (If you are living in an abusive situation, ask your pastor how you can set scriptural boundaries to protect yourself from further abuse.)

Forgiveness does not demand revenge or repayment for hurts suffered. "You mean I'm just supposed to let them off the hook?" you may argue. Yes, you let them off *your* hook, realizing that God does not let them off *His* hook. God is the just Judge who will make everything right in the end (see Romans 12:19).

So what is forgiveness? Forgiveness means deciding to live with the consequences of another person's sin. In reality, you will have to live with the consequences of his sin whether you forgive him or not. For example, imagine that someone in your youth group comes to you and says, "I have gossiped about you. Will you forgive me?" He can't take back gossip any easier than you can put toothpaste back into the tube. You're going to live with the gossip this person spread about you no matter how you respond to the gossiper.

You can either choose to live in bitterness and unforgiveness or in peace and forgiveness by deciding not to hold the offense against him. The latter, of course, is God's way.

Twelve Steps to Forgiveness

You may say, "I can't forgive this person because he hurt me so badly." Yes, the pain is real. Nobody has really forgiven someone without admitting the hurt and the hatred involved. But until you forgive that person, he will continue to hurt you because you have not released yourself from the past. Forgiveness is the only way to stop the pain.

Here are 12 steps you can use to walk through the process of forgiving someone who has hurt you. Following these steps will help you unchain yourself from the past and get on with your life:

1. *Write on a sheet of paper the names of the persons who hurt you.* Describe in writing the specific wrongs you suffered. For example: rejection, gossip, lack of love, unfairness, physical, verbal, sexual or emotional abuse or hatred. Ask the Lord to reveal to your mind specifically who you need to forgive from your heart. Some names may come to your mind that surprise you or that you have forgotten. Of the hundreds of people who have completed this list, 95 percent put father and mother as the first two. Three out of the first four names on most lists are close relatives. The two most overlooked people for these lists are God and yourself. God doesn't need to be forgiven, but we sometimes hold false expectations of God that lead us to anger or bitterness toward Him. We need to be released from those expectations and feelings we have of God. We also need to forgive ourselves for weaknesses and sins that God has long since forgiven.

2. *Face the hurt and the hate.* Write down how you feel about these people and their offenses. Remember: It is not a sin to admit the reality of your emotions. God knows exactly how you feel, whether you admit it or not. If you bury your feelings you will bypass the possibility of forgiveness. You must forgive from your heart.

3. *Realize that the cross of Christ makes forgiveness possible, fair and right.* Jesus took upon Himself all the sins of the world—including yours and those of the persons who have offended you—and He died "once for all" (Hebrews 10:10).

4. *Decide that you will bear the burden of each person's sin* (see Galatians 6:1-2). This means that you will not strike back at the person in the future by using the information about his sin against him (see Proverbs 17:9; Luke 6:27-34). We are to take the burden of offenses against us just as Christ took the burden of our sins.

5. *Decide to forgive.* Forgiveness is an act of the will, a conscious choice to let the other person off the hook and free yourself from the past. You may not feel like making this decision, but since God tells you to, you can choose to forgive. The other person may truly be in the wrong and in need of discipline or correction, but your responsibility is to let him off your hook. Make that decision now; your feelings of forgiveness will follow in time. You will gain your freedom by forgiving. If you don't forgive, you will be bound to that person.

6. *Take your list to God and pray the following: "I forgive* [name] *for* [list the offenses]." Let God bring to the surface every remembered pain. Stay with that person until every rejection, injustice, abuse, betrayal or neglect is specifically identified. Then go on to the next person. If you have felt bitter toward this person for some time, you may want to find a Christian counselor or trusted friend who will pray with you about it (see James 5:16).

7. *Destroy the list.* You are now free. Do not tell the offenders what you have done. Your forgiveness is between you and God only! The person you may need to forgive could be dead, such as a grandparent who abused you. It doesn't matter. You still need to forgive.

8. *Do not expect that your decision to forgive will result in major changes in the other persons.* Instead, pray for them (see Matthew 5:44) so that they too may find the freedom of forgiveness (see Galatians 5:1,13-14).

9. *Try to understand the people you have forgiven.* They are victims also.

10. *Expect positive results of forgiveness in you.* In time you will be able to think about the people who offended you without feeling hurt, anger or resentment. In many cases your forgiveness may result in your relationship being restored. In some cases that may not happen if they don't want the relationship restored.

11. *Thank God for the lessons you have learned and the maturity you have gained as a result of your decision to forgive the offenders* (see Romans 8:28-29).

12. *Be sure to accept your part of the blame.* Confess your failure to God and to others (see 1 John 1:9). Realize that if someone has something against you, you must go to that person (see Matthew 5:23-26).

Forgive and Be Free

One of the most inspiring stories of forgiveness is that of the late Corrie ten Boom. Corrie was a Christian Dutch woman who was imprisoned, beaten and humiliated in a Nazi concentration camp during World War II. After the war she returned to Germany to preach the good news of God's forgiveness.

At the close of a service in 1947, Corrie's message of forgiveness was put to a severe test. As people filed out of the church, one man came forward to talk to her. She recognized him immediately as one of the guards from the prison camp. She thought about his whip and his uniform with the skull and crossbones on the cap. She remembered the shame of walking naked past him with thousands of women prisoners. She remembered her sister's slow, terrible death there. Her blood seemed to freeze.

Corrie tried to avoid talking to him, hoping he wouldn't remember her. But he identified himself as a guard at the camp where she had been. He said, "Since that time I have become a Christian. I know that God has forgiven me for the cruel things I did there." Then he stuck out his hand. "Will you forgive me?"

She stood there with coldness clutching her heart. She did not want to forgive him. She didn't feel like forgiving him. But she knew forgiveness is an act of the will, not an emotion. "Jesus, help me!" she prayed silently. "I can lift my hand. I can do that much. You supply the feeling."

Almost mechanically she reached out to grasp his hand. As they joined hands, a healing warmth seemed to flood her whole being, bringing tears to her eyes. "I forgive you, brother!" she cried. "With my whole heart!"

The former guard and the former prisoner grasped each other's hands for a long moment. Forgiveness had healed the hurts of the past.[1]

When we forgive, we throw off the chains of bitterness and start the process of healing those damaged emotions. We are no longer bound by our past. By forgiving and setting the other person free, we find that we have really set ourselves free.

TRUTH ENCOUNTER

1. Name one area where you need God's help in dealing with your past. What action(s) do you need to take?
2. What is forgiveness?
3. Why isn't forgiving the same as forgetting?
4. Will you choose to forgive those who have hurt you? What will happen if you don't?

Note
1. Adapted from a tract by Good News Publishers, Westchester, Illinois.

DEALING WITH REJECTION IN YOUR RELATIONSHIPS

"Thoughts and feelings of rejection and criticism can cripple our growth in Christ if we don't learn to handle them the right way."

One night, 19-year-old Sean Sellers, a Satan worshiper, took a gun into his parents' bedroom and shot them to death as they slept. Sellers admitted that satanism and the occult played a large role in the tragedy. But there was more to the story than his experience with the dark side of life. Sellers felt rejected and alone. He stated that if he had had a close family relationship, he might never have become involved in satanism.

We can't excuse Sean Sellers's actions simply because he felt rejected. But the fact remains that his failure to deal with feelings of rejection, whether real or imagined, contributed to his horrible crime.

Most of us haven't suffered the extreme rejection that Sean Sellers described. But everyone knows what it feels like to be criticized and rejected at times, even by the very people in our lives we desperately want to please. We were born and raised in a worldly surrounding that chooses favorites and rejects seconds. And since nobody can be the best at everything, we all were ignored, overlooked or rejected at times by parents, teachers and friends.

Furthermore, since we were born in sin, even God rejected us until we were accepted by Him in Christ at salvation (see Romans 15:7). Since then we have been the target of Satan, the accuser (see Revelation 12:10), who never stops lying to us about how worthless we are to God and others. In this life we all have to live with the pain and pressure of rejection.

WHEN YOU ARE CRITICIZED OR REJECTED

Thoughts and feelings of rejection and criticism can cripple our growth in Christ if we don't learn to handle them the right way.

Unfortunately, instead of taking a positive approach, we all learned early in life to respond to rejection by taking one of three defensive positions.

Beat the System

Some people defend against rejection by buying into the dog-eat-dog system and learning to compete and scheme to get ahead of the pack. These are the kids on campus who earn acceptance and strive for importance through their performance. They feel driven to get on top of every situation because winning is their passport to acceptance. They are determined to beat the system, to win at all costs. They are characterized by striving to do everything right, not letting anyone get close to them personally, worrying and being stressed out most of the time.

Spiritually, the beat-the-system individual refuses to come under God's authority and has little fellowship with God. This person is committed to controlling and manipulating people and circumstances for his own purposes. It is difficult for him to yield control to God. In the youth group this person schemes to be chairman of the ruling youth board or the most influential member on a committee. His motivation is not to serve God in this position, however, but to control his world because his self-worth depends on it. Beat-the-system controllers are some of the most insecure people you will meet.

Sadly, the controlling individual's defensive strategy only creates more rejection. Others soon begin to resent him for his self-centered living.

Give in to the System

"Pastor, I'm a loser," a high schooler told me (Neil) dejectedly. He explained that he wanted to be a star football player, but had been cut from the team. Instead of being in the spotlight as an athlete, he had to settle for being a member of the pep band. And compared to star quarterbacks, clarinet players were considered losers.

Many young people respond to the unfairness of this worldly system like this teen did: by simply giving in to it. They continue their efforts to try to satisfy others, but their failures drive them to believe that they really are unlovable and rejectable. The system says that the best, the strongest, the most beautiful and the most talented are "in." Those who don't fit those categories—which includes most of us—are "out," and we buy into society's false judgment of our worth. As a result, a large number of high schoolers and junior highers are plagued with feelings of worthlessness, inferiority and self-condemnation.

This person also has trouble relating to God. He often blames God for his condition and finds it difficult to trust Him. "You made me a lowly clarinet player instead of a star quarterback," he complains. "If I open up other areas of my life to You, how do I know You won't make me a loser there too?"

By giving in to the system's false judgment, this person can only look forward to more and more rejection. He has bought the lie and even rejects himself. Therefore any success or acceptance that comes his way will be questioned or doubted on the basis of what he already believes about himself.

Rebel Against the System

The rebels and the dropouts take this position. They respond to a godless world system by saying, "I don't need you or your love." Deep inside they still crave acceptance, but they refuse to admit their need. They will often show their rebellion by dressing and behaving in ways that often send their parents through the roof.

The rebel is marked by self-hatred and bitterness. She wishes she had never been born. She is irresponsible and undisciplined. She sees God as just another tyrant, someone else trying to squeeze her into a socially acceptable mold. She rebels against God just like she rebels against everyone else.

This person's rebellious attitude and behavior tend to alienate others and push them to defend the system she rejects. Therefore the rebel's response to those who reject her just breeds more rejection.

Get Defensive

As long as we live on planet Earth we will experience rejection from others. How should we respond to it? Should we try to defend ourselves? No. There are two reasons why you never need to be defensive when the world is critical of you.

First, if you are in the wrong, you don't *have* a defense. Let's say that you do something wrong and are criticized for it. If you make excuses and try to defend yourself, you're deceiving yourself.

You must simply respond, "You're right; I was wrong," then take steps to improve your character and change your behavior.

Second, if you are right, you don't *need a* defense. Peter encouraged us to follow in the footsteps of Jesus who "While being reviled, He did not revile in return; while suffering, He uttered no threats, but kept entrusting Himself to Him who judges righteously" (1 Peter 2:23). If you are in the right, you don't need to defend yourself. God, the Righteous Judge, who knows who you are and what you have done, will defend you.

If you can learn not to be defensive when someone exposes your weaknesses or attacks your performance, you may have a chance to turn the situation around and minister to that person. You don't have to respond to rejection by beating the system, giving in to the system or rebelling against the system. The world's system for determining your value as a person is not what determines your value. Your allegiance is to Christ your lord, not to the world. If you find yourself responding to rejection defensively, let it remind you to focus your attention on those things that will build up and establish your faith.

WHEN YOU ARE TEMPTED TO CRITICIZE OR REJECT OTHERS

Rejection is a two-way street: You can receive it and you can give it. We've talked about how to respond to the rejection you receive within the world's system. Now let's look at how to respond to the temptation to tear up others with criticism or rejection.

Let's imagine that two friends, Kevin and Kelly, are at a table in McDonald's. They're in the middle of a blazing argument. They wail away at each other verbally, slamming one another with insults and accusations and calling each other every name in the book.

Now imagine that I (Dave) am their youth pastor, and I see them chewing each other to pieces. "Time out!" I say. We order a round of Cokes and drink them while Kevin and Kelly cool down. Then I pull out a sheet of paper and ask the two friends to open their Bibles, which, of course, they have with them. I draw a simple diagram (see Figure 12) to help them see their argument in the light of God's Word.

FIGURE 12

YOU ARE RESPONSIBLE FOR:

YOUR OWN
CHARACTER

YOUR OWN
CHARACTER

EACH
OTHER'S
NEEDS

I ask Kevin to read Romans 14:4. He finds it and reads, "Who are you to judge the servant of another? To his own master he stands or falls; and stand he will, for the Lord is able to make him stand." Then I say, "That verse is talking about judging another person's character. Before God, each of you is responsible for your own character." Kevin and Kelly nod their agreement, still glaring at each other.

At my request, Kelly next reads Philippians 2:3: "Do nothing from selfishness or empty conceit, but with humility of mind let each of you regard one another as more important than himself."

"That verse is talking about needs," I continue. "Before God, each of you is responsible for meeting each other's needs." Again Kevin and Kelly agree with my statement.

Then I say, "Do you realize what you have been doing during your argument? Instead of taking responsibility for your own character, you've been ripping apart each other's character. Instead of looking out for your friend's needs, you've been selfishly absorbed with your own needs. No wonder you're chewing each other out."

Since Kevin and Kelly are both sensitive, intelligent people, they prayerfully commit to refocus their friendship according to God's Word.

What about your relationships? Are you treating those around you like your brothers or sisters and your friends? Are you focusing on your character development or are you attacking the character of others? Are you trying to meet the needs of others around you or are you just a taker that never gives?

What kind of families and youth groups would we have if we all assumed responsibility for our own character and sought to meet the needs of those we live with? They would be almost heavenly. But instead of devoting ourselves to developing our own character and meeting each other's needs, we often yield to Satan's prodding to criticize each other's character and selfishly meet our own needs. We will only encourage each other to grow up in Christ if we practice what God's Word says.

Focus on Responsibilities

Another way Satan has deceived us in our relationships is by tempting us to focus on our rights instead of our responsibilities. For example, a teen may get upset with his parent because he feels he has a right to stay out as late as he wants. But in God's system, our focus is to fulfill our responsibilities, not insist on our rights. Staying out late is not your right; but being a loving, obedient son or daughter is your responsibility. When we stand before Christ, He will not ask us if we received everything we had coming to us. But He will reward us for how well we fulfilled our responsibilities.

Don't Play the Role of Conscience

Sometimes we are tempted to play the role of the Holy Spirit or the conscience in someone else's life on issues where the Scriptures are not crystal clear: "Christians shouldn't drink or smoke"; "You should spend at least 30 minutes a day in prayer"; "You should study your Bible every day."

The Holy Spirit knows exactly when to bring conviction on issues of conscience. It's part of the process of growing to Christian maturity that He directs. When we attempt to play His role, we often do little more than display criticism and rejection. Our job is to surround people with acceptance and let the Holy Spirit do His job in His time.

Discipline Yes, Judgment No

Are there any times when we should confront each other because of the way we act? Yes. We are required by God to confront and restore Christians who have clearly violated the boundaries of Scripture (see Matthew 18:15-16). We are instructed to confront others concerning sins we have observed, but we are not allowed to judge their character (see Matthew 7:1; Romans 14:13). Disciplining behavior is our job; judging character is God's job.

For example, imagine that you just caught your sister telling a lie. "You're a liar," you say to her. That's judgment, an attack on her character. But if you say, "Sis, you just told a lie," you are not judging her; you're holding her accountable for behavior you observed.

Or suppose you see a Christian friend cheating on an exam at school. If you call him a cheater, you are judging his character. You can only confront him on the basis of what you see: "By cheating on your exam you are getting a grade you don't deserve, and that's wrong."

When you confront someone, it must be based on something you have personally seen or heard, not on something you suspect or have heard about through the grapevine. If you confront his behavior and he does not respond to you, then bring two or three witnesses to his sin. If you are the only eyewitness, you confront him alone and leave it at that. Every time he sees you, God will remind him of his sin. Eventually he will either get right or break off his relationship with you.

Much of what some call discipline is nothing less than character assassination. We say to failing Christian brothers and sisters, "You're not a good Christian"; "You're a cheater"; "You're a sex pervert." Such statements don't correct or build up; they tear down character and show disapproval for the person as well as her problem. Your Christian friend is not a cheater; she's a child of God who has taken grades that don't belong to her. The believer caught in sexual sin is not a pervert; he's a child of God who compromised his purity. We must care enough about people to confront their sinful behavior, but we should never tear down their character.

Express Your Needs Without Judging

Is it okay to express our personal needs to others? Yes, if you don't slam others in the process. For example, you feel unloved in a relationship, so you say, "You don't love me anymore." Or you say to

your mom or dad, "You make me feel worthless." Or you feel a distance developing between you and your friend, so you say, "You
never write or call."

You think you have expressed your need, but you have
slammed the other person in the process. When you push off your
need as someone else's problem, he will probably respond by getting defensive, further straining the relationship.

What if you expressed your needs this way: "I need to feel
loved by you"; "I need your affirmation and your support";
"I miss it when we don't write or call regularly." By changing the
"you" accusation to an "I" message, you express your need without
blaming anyone. Your nonjudgmental approach allows God to deal
with the person's conscience and turns a potential problem into an
opportunity for ministry. The other person is free to respond to
your need instead of defending himself against your attack.

We all have basic human needs to feel loved, accepted and
worthwhile. When these needs go unmet, it's very important that
we express them to our family members and fellow Christians in a
positive way and allow others to minister to those needs.

The basis for all temptation is real needs that are not being
met. When you are too proud to say, "I don't feel loved," or when
you push others away by saying, "You don't love me anymore," your
need for love goes unmet. So Satan comes along with a tempting
alternative. Your mom and dad don't love you the way you need to
be loved, so you begin to think about running away. When you fail
to express your needs in a proper way, you make yourself a target
for temptation.

One of the main resources God uses for meeting our needs
and keeping us pure is other believers. The problem is that many
of us go to Sunday School, church and youth group wearing a
mask. Wanting to appear strong and together, we rob ourselves of
the opportunity of having our needs met in the warmth and safety of a group of Christians; in the process, we rob the group of the
opportunity to minister to our needs—one of the main reasons
God gathered us into churches. By not letting other believers meet
our legitimate needs, we are acting independently of God and we
are vulnerable to the world, the flesh and the devil.

We all know that following Christ involves both the vertical
and the horizontal—loving God and loving people. It is important
to know that God works in our lives through committed relation-

ships. Where better to learn patience, kindness, forgiveness and team spirit than in the close quarters of Christian relationships?

Anybody can find character defects and performance flaws in another Christian. But it takes the grace of God to look beyond a foot-in-mouth Peter to see in him the rock of the Jerusalem church. It takes the grace of God to look beyond Saul the persecutor to see in him Paul the apostle. So as we live day to day with people who are sometimes less than saintly in their behavior—and who see us the same way—may we simply say, "Grace and peace be multiplied to you" (2 Peter 1:2).

TRUTH ENCOUNTER

1. How have you responded in a wrong way to others, either by being critical or defensive?
2. Why do you never need to respond defensively when someone is critical of you?
3. What should you do if you are tempted to criticize or reject someone?
4. Why do you think Satan would like you to focus on your rights instead of your responsibilities?

PEOPLE GROW BETTER TOGETHER

*"We have the awesome privilege and responsibility
to be both teachers and learners of what it means to be
in Christ, walk in the Spirit and live by faith."*

If you play any kind of team sport like football, baseball, basketball, soccer or volleyball, you are keenly aware of the importance of teamwork. It's not much fun playing these games alone. You can't play all the positions by yourself. You can't cover all the bases. Being part of a well-coached, tightly knit team is the only way to compete and win in team sports.

God has designed His church to be a team as well. As Christians, we need each other. It's tough living the Christian life. The temptations of the world, the flesh and the devil distract us from our walk with Christ. The pressure to make right choices among worldly friends is great. Alone we tend to get discouraged, like one player competing against nine on a baseball diamond. But together we find strength as we encourage each other, pray for each other and build each other up.

A good place for you to find the togetherness, support and team spirit you need is in a church, specifically a group of kids your age who study the Bible together, pray together and serve God together. The youth group is not just a gathering of friends. It's an environment where you can become deeply involved in the lives of other Christian teens. It's a place of trust where you can share your concerns, a place where people really care about you and support you for who you are in Christ. It's a place where you and your Christian friends can help each other grow as disciples of Jesus Christ.

DISCIPLESHIP: THE HEARTBEAT OF GROWTH AND MATURITY

Discipleship is the intensely personal activity of two or more persons helping each other experience a growing relationship with God. Every Christian is both a disciple and a discipler in his Christian relationships. We have the awesome privilege and responsibility to be both teachers and learners of what it means to be in Christ, walk in the Spirit and live by faith. We are always learning and growing in Christ through our relationships. And we always have the opportunity to help our friends and other believers grow in Christ through our caring, committed relationship with them.

In the same way, every Christian has the opportunity to be a peer counselor and to receive counsel in his Christian relationships. How much you have grown in the Lord will determine how much counseling you do. But no matter how much you have grown, there will still be times when you need to seek or receive counsel from other Christians. You may be a new Christian or come from a problem-filled past, and you are still receiving a good deal of counseling. You also need to be alert to opportunities God will give you to offer helpful advice to other believers around you.

The following designs for discipleship and concepts for counseling will give you some practical guidelines for your ministry to others.

DESIGNS FOR DISCIPLESHIP

There are three levels in the ministry of discipling others given by Paul in Colossians 2:6-10. The levels of discipleship are summarized in Figure 13A.

Level I relates to helping people with the basic issues of establishing and understanding their *identity* in Christ. Paul declared the finished work of who we are in Christ: "In Him you have been made complete" (Colossians 2:10).

Level II deals with the issue of *maturity* in Christ, which Paul called "being built up in Him" (Colossians 2:7).

Level III reflects the issue of our daily *walk* in Christ, which is founded on our identity and maturity. Paul instructed, "As you therefore have received Christ Jesus the Lord, so walk in Him" (Colossians 2:6).

DISCIPLING IN CHRIST

LEVELS OF CONFLICT AND GROWTH

	LEVEL I: IDENTITY Complete in Christ (Colossians 2:10)	LEVEL II: MATURITY Built up in Christ (Colossians 2:7)	LEVEL III: WALK Walk in Christ (Colossians 2:6)
SPIRITUAL LIFE	Conflict: Lack of salvation or assurance (Ephesians 2:1-3)	Conflict: Walking according to the flesh (Galatians 5:19-21)	Conflict: Insensitive to the Spirit's leading (Hebrews 5:11-14)
	Growth: Child of God (1 John 3:1-3; 5:11-13)	Growth: Walking according to the Spirit (Galatians 5:22-23)	Growth: Led by the Spirit (Romans 8:14)
MIND	Conflict: Darkened under- standing (Ephesians 4:18)	Conflict: Wrong beliefs or philosophy of life (Colossians 2:8)	Conflict: Pride (1 Corinthians 8:1)
	Growth: Renewed mind (Romans 12:2; Ephesians 4:23)	Growth: Handling accurately the Word of Truth (2 Timothy 2:15)	Growth: Adequate, equipped for every good work (2 Timothy 3:16-17)

	LEVEL I:	LEVEL II:	LEVEL III:
EMOTIONS	**Conflict:** Fear (Matthew 10:26-33)	**Conflict:** Anger (Ephesians 4:31), anxiety (1 Peter 5:7), depression (2 Corinthians 4:1-18)	**Conflict:** Discouragement and sorrow (Galatians 6:9)
	Growth: Freedom (Galatians 5:1)	**Growth:** Joy, peace, patience (Galatians 5:22)	**Growth:** Contentment (Philippians 4:11)
WILL	**Conflict:** Rebellion (1 Timothy 1:9)	**Conflict:** Lack of self-control, compulsive (1 Corinthians 3:1-3)	**Conflict:** Undisciplined (2 Thessalonians 3:7,11)
	Growth: Submissive (Romans 13:1-2)	**Growth:** Self-control (Galatians 5:23)	**Growth:** Disciplined (1 Timothy 4:7-8)
RELATION-SHIPS	**Conflict:** Rejection (Ephesians 2:1-3)	**Conflict:** Unforgiveness (Colossians 3:1-3)	**Conflict:** Selfishness (Philippians 2:1-5; 1 Corinthians 10:24)
	Growth: Acceptance (Romans 5:8; 15:7)	**Growth:** Forgiveness (Ephesians 4:32)	**Growth:** Brotherly love (Romans 12:10; Philippians 2:1-5)

Each level is dependent on the former level for success. A Christian cannot have an effective walk (Level III) if she is not moving into maturity (Level II), and she cannot approach maturity if she is not first rooted in Christ (Level I).

Notice also that there are five areas of application for each level: spiritual life, mind, emotions, will and relationships. In each area there is both a point of conflict and a step of growth. The point of conflict identifies how sin, the world, the flesh and the devil interfere in the discipleship process. The points of conflict indicate what must be resolved and replaced by specific steps of growth.

Level 1: Identity

Spiritual life. The point of spiritual conflict on Level I is the individual's lack of salvation (if he has *not* been born again) or lack of assurance of salvation (if he *has* been born again). It's not our job to give assurance of salvation; God does that (see Romans 8:16; 1 John 5:13). Our role in this step of growth is to lead people to Christ and show them Scriptures that declare their spiritual identity as children of God.

Mind. People come into the kingdom of God having little or no true knowledge of Him. People must have a knowledge of God in order to believe God and be what He wants them to be (see Hosea 4:6). Unless their minds are renewed and they develop a proper belief system, they will attempt to meet basic needs in the wrong way: independently of God.

Emotions. The emotional problem at this level is fear. Fear drives people to do what they should not do and prevents them from doing what they should do. When people are motivated by the fear of anyone or anything except God, they are not free, and freedom is our inheritance in Christ. Satan binds through fear, but the fear of God expels all other fears.

Will. Most people want to rebel against those in authority over them: God, parents, teachers, police, and so forth. Growth in this area involves learning how to submit to God and to others in authority.

Relationships. Since acceptance in the world is based on how well we perform, most people have experienced rejection from childhood. Yet the kingdom of God is based on God's unconditional love and acceptance (see Titus 3:5). We must also build our relationships on love and acceptance, not judgment.

The first goal of discipleship is to establish identity in Christ. This entails:

1. Leading individuals to Christ and directing them to their scriptural assurance of salvation;
2. Guiding them to a true knowledge of God and who they are in Christ, and starting them down the path of knowing God's ways;
3. Changing their basic motivation from fear of people and circumstances to fear of God;
4. Helping them see the ways they are still playing God or rebelling against God's authority;
5. Breaking down their defenses against rejection by loving and accepting them.

Level 2: Maturity

Spiritual life. Building people up to Christ begins in the spiritual area by helping them to learn the difference between walking according to the flesh and walking according to the Spirit. The more they choose to walk according to the flesh, the longer they will remain immature. The more they choose to walk according to the Spirit, the sooner they will mature.

Mind. When Christians buy into Stan's lie or worldly ideas, they will not be able to grow (see Colossians 2:8). The battle is for the mind, and we must learn to expose Satan's strategies and take every thought captive (see 2 Corinthians 10:5). Discipleship requires mental discipline. People who will not take responsibility for their thoughts cannot be discipled.

Emotions. Feelings are a product of the thought life. If a person's thoughts and beliefs are wrong concerning what will make her successful, important or happy, she will experience negative emotions. Anger, anxiety and depression are usually the result of a false belief system. Mental and emotional health are largely the byproduct of a true knowledge of God, an acceptance of His ways and the assurance of His forgiveness.

Will. In order to mature, Christians must choose to exercise self-control instead of giving in to the desires of the flesh.

Relationships. Forgiveness is the key to maturity. It is the glue that holds families and youth groups together. Satan uses unforgiveness to stop the growth of individuals and ministries. The unforgiving person is tied to his painful past or to a person who hurt him and is not free to move on in Christ.

The second goal of discipleship is to accept God's goal to grow in Christlikeness. This means:

1. Helping people learn to walk by the Spirit and by faith;
2. Guiding them to discipline their minds to believe the truth;
3. Helping them get off the emotional roller coaster by focusing their thoughts on God instead of their circumstances;
4. Encouraging them to develop self-control;
5. Challenging them to resolve personal problems by forgiving others and seeking forgiveness.

Level 3: Walk

So many Christians want to start their journey of discipleship at this level instead of at Levels I and II. They ask, "What should I *do* to grow as a Christian?" when they should be asking, "Who should I *be*?" We can't expect people to behave as mature Christians (Level III) before they have matured as Christians (Levels I and II). However, as believers affirm their identity in Christ and grow in maturity, we can further disciple them by challenging them to consistent Christlike behavior in their daily walk.

Spiritual life. Spiritually mature people have learned to tell the difference between good and evil (see Hebrews 5:14). This is called "spiritual discernment." Through His Spirit, God helps mature believers recognize thoughts and activities that are being suggested by Satan. Spiritual discernment is the first line of defense in spiritual warfare.

Mind. The believer will never know so much of God and his ways that he no longer needs God. If Christians get to the place where they lean on their own understanding, they will stop acknowledging God. The honest student of God's Word must admit that the more he knows about God, the more dependent he must be upon Him.

Emotions. The mature believer learns to be content in all circumstances (see Philippians 4:11). There are a lot of discouragements in this life, and many of the believer's desires will go unmet. But none of his goals will go unfulfilled as long as they are godly goals.

Will. Someone has said that the successful Christian life depends on the exercise of the will. The undisciplined person is unable to live a productive life. But the disciplined person is a Spirit-filled person who has no unresolved problems and who seeks to have his needs met in Christ.

Relationships. The mature believer no longer lives for herself but for others. Perhaps the greatest test of the believer's maturity is found in the call to "be devoted to one another in brotherly love" (Romans 12:10). After all, the world will not recognize us as true Christians by the youth group we attend, our Christian school, our appearance or our athletic trophies, but by our love.

Simply stated, the third goal of discipleship is to help believers function as believers in their homes, their schools, their youth groups and society. The effective Christian walk involves the proper exercise of spiritual gifts and talents in serving others and being a positive witness in the world. These standards are only valid when an individual accepts her identity and experiences maturity in Christ.

Sadly, most Christian teaching and preaching to youth is directed at Level III, hoping to produce better behavior. But most young Christians are stuck down around Level I, locked into the past, immobilized by fear, isolated by rejection. They have no idea who they are in Christ, so they have no way of succeeding at the Christian walk. Rather than continually telling immature believers what they should *do*, let's celebrate with them what Christ has already *done* and help them become who they already are in Him.

CONCEPTS FOR COUNSELING

Would you be willing to commit yourself to become the kind of person someone could confide in? That's essentially what a peer counselor is: a person with whom others feel confident in sharing the problems of their present and past. Being able to counsel someone doesn't require that you be 18 or older or have a college degree, although those who counsel professionally can be greatly helped by receiving Bible-based training. God can use you to encourage and instruct youth with problems if you are a compassionate, caring person.

Counseling seeks to help people deal with the present by resolving problems from the past. The goal of Christian counseling—whether done by a youth pastor, a professional counselor or a caring friend—is to help people experience freedom in Christ so that they can move on to maturity and fruitfulness in their walk with Him. Here are five practical tips for the informal peer counseling God may lead you to do within your Christian relationships.

1. Help People Identify Root Issues

Psalm 1:1-3 compares the mature Christian to a fruitful tree (see Figure 13B). The fruitfulness of the branches above the ground is the result of the fertility of the soil and the health of the root system that spreads into it. Ideally, the believer is planted in the fertile soil of his identity in Christ (Level I), spreads out his roots of maturity (Level II) and bears the fruit of a productive walk in Christ (Level III).

People usually seek counseling because something is wrong with their daily walk. Instead of being fruitful, their lives are barren. As with a tree, more times than not the surface problem is only the symptom of a deeper issue. Their branches are dry and barren because there is something wrong with the root system and they are not feeding on the nourishment in the soil.

The first goal in counseling is to help the person identify the root cause for his unfruitful walk. To do this, it is helpful to determine which of his needs are not being met and how he is trying to meet those needs. His comments to you will tip off his unmet needs. For example, if he says, "I feel out of place everywhere; nobody loves me," he needs acceptance and belonging. If he says, "I'm just a loser; I'm no good," his needs for identity and worth are going unmet. If he says, "My life is falling apart; I'm depressed," he needs security and hope. If he says, "I can't do anything right," he feels incompetent. If he says, "I can't stop what I'm doing," he needs freedom.

In order to expose his root problem, you need to help him work through several critical questions within the five areas illustrated in Figure 13A. The questions below should not be asked to the person directly because he may not know the answers. But they are questions you need to keep in mind as you talk with him.

Emotions. The emotional level is a good place to start because your friend's negative feelings are probably what brought him to you for advice. Try to understand: When did he begin to feel this way? What events surrounded that experience? What does he think about the event? What unfulfilled "goals" do his feelings reveal?

Mind. What does he believe about God? About himself? About success in life? Guiding the person through the Belief Quiz (see chapter 7) will help him discover his present belief system.

COLOSSIANS 2:6-7

BARREN LIFE

REJECTION

REBELLION

FEAR

UNFORGIVENESS

FALSE BELIEF SYSTEM

FRUITFUL LIFE

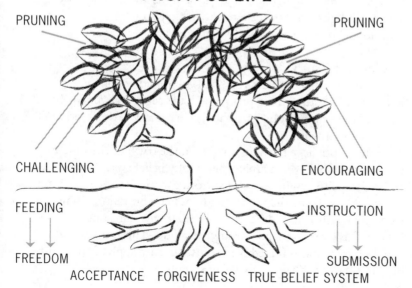

PRUNING

PRUNING

CHALLENGING

ENCOURAGING

FEEDING

INSTRUCTION

FREEDOM

SUBMISSION

ACCEPTANCE   FORGIVENESS   TRUE BELIEF SYSTEM

Will. How does he respond to authority? In what ways is he playing God? Is he responsible to a youth pastor or a local church? Is he weak-willed, unable to say no or to stand alone? Does he believe he is controlled by life's events? Is he undisciplined? Does he act without thinking?

Relationships. What expectations does he have of God and others? Who does he need to forgive? From whom does he need to seek forgiveness? What people skills does he lack? Does he have a support system (family, friends, youth group)?

Spiritual life. What is his present standing with God? Does he know how to walk according to the Spirit? Is he sensitive to the Holy Spirit's leading? Does he have a quiet time with God consisting of prayer and Bible study?

2. Encourage Emotional Honesty

People are generally willing to share what has happened to them, but they are not usually willing to share their failures or how they feel about them. Unless you can encourage them to emotional honesty, their chances of solving their inner problems are slim. You cannot be right with God and not be real emotionally.

When a Christian keeps his emotions in the dark by not sharing them honestly, he gives Satan a foothold. When a person honestly admits how he feels in an attempt to solve his problems, he exposes his soul to God's light. Satan and his demons are like cockroaches. When the light invades their territory, they run for the shadows. Emotional honesty keeps the devil on the run.

3. Share the Truth

When your Christian friends come to you for advice or counseling, it's usually because their problems have caused them to think there is something wrong with them. They may feel that God can't possibly love them.

What a privilege to share with them the truth of their identity in Christ and help them repair their faulty belief system. Keep several copies of the "Who Am I?" list from chapter 2 and "Since I Am in Christ" list from chapter 3 handy. When you talk to someone who reveals distorted ideas about himself, give him one of those lists and ask him to read through it aloud. The transformation you'll see in people is incredible because they are applying the truth of God's Word to their faulty belief system.

4. Call for a Response

Your role in advising and counseling your friends is to share the truth in love and pray that they will choose to accept it. But you cannot choose for them. Good scriptural advice must be received by faith.

Our Lord said to those seeking His healing touch, "Your faith has made you well; go in peace and be healed of your affliction" (Mark 5:34); "Go; it shall be done for you as you have believed" (Matthew 8:13). If those you share with don't want help or choose to not believe, there isn't much you can do to help them.

The response we desire in our peer counseling is that of repentance, which means a changing of the mind. The person seeking help needs to change his mind about what he will believe about God and himself. Only after he changes his mind and changes his beliefs can he change his walk.

5. Help Them Plan for the Future

One of the most important ways to help people move from problems and despair to growth, maturity and hope is to help them develop a support system of relationships. Encourage them to rely on the prayers, fellowship and instruction they receive in a loving family, a youth group or a cluster of close Christian friends.

Help your friends see the difference between what is and what can be in their lives. Change in belief and behavior takes time. People need to realize the important difference between goals and desires, or they will try to change things and people that are beyond their right or ability to change. Encourage your friends to face each day of growth with the attitude expressed in the popular prayer, "God grant me the serenity to accept the things I cannot change, the courage to change the things I can, and the wisdom to know the difference."

We are what we are by the grace of God. All we have and can hope for—as disciplers and disciples, as counselors and people in need of counsel—is based on who we are in Christ. May your life and your ministry to others be shaped by your devotion to Christ and the conviction that He is the way, the truth and the life (see John 14:6). And may God grant us all the privilege of seeing people escape the shadows and mature in the light.

TRUTH ENCOUNTER

1. Why is it so important that you be a part of a youth group?
2. Why should we celebrate who a person is in Christ, rather than tell him what he does is wrong?
3. Why is emotional honesty so important?
4. What is a good balance between being a good disciple and a discipler?

STOMPING OUT THE DARKNESS

SMALL-GROUP STUDY GUIDE

A NOTE FROM NEIL AND DAVE

In Luke 5:1-11, Jesus was instructing the multitudes from Peter's boat: "And when He had finished speaking, He said to Simon, 'Put out into the deep water and let down your nets for a catch'" (v. 4). Jesus had stopped talking, but He had not stopped teaching. Peter heard what Jesus said, but he hadn't learned until he got into the boat and put out the nets.

This study guide gives you an opportunity to get into the boat and put out the nets. You can do it alone, but we recommend that you do it with other faithful learners. It provides an opportunity for more collective wisdom, and greater learning always takes place in the context of committed relationships. Developing trusting relationships and being devoted to one another in prayer is what makes group study so enriching.

We are thankful for the tremendous work that Lisa Guest, who also developed the study guide for *The Bondage Breaker Youth Edition* (Harvest House, 1995), has done in putting together this study guide. Another helpful resource is *Busting Free!* (Gospel Light, 1994), a curriculum for teaching these truths in a Sunday School class or small group. A summary of some of the resources available from Discipleship Counseling Ministries (www.discipleshipcounsel ingministries.org) and Freedom in Christ Ministries (info@ficm.org) is given at the end of this study guide.

It is our prayer that you will fully realize who you are in Christ and learn to live as a child of God. If this study guide helps make that possible, we will be thankful. May the grace and love of our heavenly Father bless you with all of the riches of your inheritance in Christ.

Neil T. Anderson
Dave Park

WHO ARE YOU?

We can't point a bony finger at you, but we can and are going to ask you, "Who are you?" Start from the outside but work down to the core. Get beyond what you look like and what you do (those are good enough starting points) to who you'd still be if you lost those externals.

Is who we are determined by what we do, or is what we do determined by who we are? Read that question again slowly and then decide if it's one or the other or both—and explain why you think so.

We (Neil and Dave) think that what we do is determined by who we are, and that's why we really want you to get to know who you are in Christ. So let's get to it!

WHEN THE OUTSIDE AND INSIDE DON'T ADD UP

The world offers the following equations as paths to identity and meaning, to belonging and significance:

> Appearance + Accomplishments + Recognition = Peace
> Good looks + Popularity = Wholeness
> Star performances + Great accomplishments = Happiness

- Which of the above equations, if any, best describes how you're living life?

- When have you seen—for yourself or in a friend's life—that these equations are false? More specifically, when have you felt for yourself or seen in someone else's life that:

> Appearance + Accomplishments + Recognition ≠ Peace
> Good looks + Popularity ≠ Wholeness
> Star performances + Great accomplishments ≠ Happiness
> Success ≠ Contentment
> Failure ≠ Hopelessness

The world's math is all wrong. The only identity equation that works in God's kingdom is: You + Christ = Wholeness and Meaning.

- If our identity in Christ is the key to wholeness, why do you think so many believers have difficulty with self-worth, spiritual growth and maturity?

- Why would the devil want to deceive us about our true identity in Christ? What can he accomplish by keeping us down on ourselves and unsure about whether we're worth anything?

Too often, Satan tricks us into believing that what we do (failing, sinning) makes us what we are (failures, sinners). This false belief sinks us deeper and deeper into the muddy pit of hopelessness and defeat. The only way out of that pit is to get a grip on who you really are as God's child.

THE GOOD THINGS WE INHERITED FROM FATHER ADAM

In order to understand who we really are, we need to understand what traits we inherited—good and bad—from Adam at Creation. For starters, just like Adam, we have physical bodies and inner selves, sometimes called souls, which are the parts of us created in God's image.

Physically Alive. Like Adam, we walk around in a living, breathing earth suit made up of skin, muscle, bone, blood, fat and hair.

- What does 2 Corinthians 5:1-4 suggest about the relationship between your body and your soul?

- Your soul is eternal, but your body is guaranteed for only one lifetime. What does this fact say to you about your efforts to find significance through having the "right"-sized biceps or waistline, the "right" clothes and the "right" haircut?

Spiritually Alive. We are spiritually alive when our inner selves are united with God. After all, we were created to be in relationship with God. But Adam sinned and his relationship with God—and ours as well—was broken. That's why we were born spiritually dead and why Christ died on the cross.

- When did you first become aware that you were spiritually dead? What happened in your life? What did you do after you realized your sin and your distance from God? What do you do to keep yourself close to God now?

- Maybe you're just now starting to think about your spiritual health. What sins are you becoming aware of? What emptiness are you noticing inside?

If you have come to a point of recognizing that you need God's forgiveness, tell Him that. Ask Him to forgive your sins (be specific) and thank Him for sending His Son, Jesus, to pay the penalty for those sins by dying on the cross (see John 3:10). Invite Jesus to become Lord of your life and ask God to help you learn more about how to live a life that pleases Him (see Romans 10:9-10).

Significance. We all want to be significant or important, and from the start Adam was extremely significant.

- According to Genesis 1:26-27, what purpose for living did God give Adam?

- Satan stole Adam's significance (and ours) when Adam sinned, but Jesus won it back for us through His death and His resurrection. Explain what Josh McDowell means when he writes, "You are 'worth Jesus' to God" (page 14).

- The price that God paid for you is Jesus Christ. What purpose for living has God given you? (See the "Strength Givers" at this end of this lesson.)

- What does knowing that God has called you to be light and salt do to your negative thoughts about yourself?

Safety and Security. Before Adam sinned in the garden, he enjoyed a sense of safety and security. He lacked nothing.

- In Christ, we inherit safety and security as well as significance. What long-term safety and security does God offer you, His child? (See Romans 8:38-39 and 1 John 1:9.)

- When in your day-to-day life have you felt the safety and security God gives?

- What does Philippians 4:19 mean to you personally? (Note that Paul talks about our needs, not our wants. Those are two different lists!)

Belonging. Adam and Eve experienced a sense of belonging. First Adam enjoyed an intimate relationship with God. Then, when God gave Eve to Adam—and Adam to Eve—he experienced a different sense of belonging.

- When has your relationship with God, made possible because of Christ, given you a sense of belonging?

- What relationships with people give you a sense of belonging?

- How does the belonging you feel in relationships with Christian friends compare to the belonging you feel in other relationships?

THE BAD THINGS WE INHERITED FROM FATHER ADAM

Just as we received good things from Adam, we also received negative side effects from his fall. Below each side effect, note evidence of this inheritance that you've found in your own life.

Spiritual Death. When Adam and Eve sinned, they were separated from God—and that is spiritual death. List some of the evidence of your separation from God:

_____
_____
_____
_____
_____

Lost Knowledge of God. With their sin, Adam and Eve lost their true understanding of God as well as their ability to love God and experience a deep friendship and intimacy with Him. List some of the evidence of your distance from God and your inability to love Him:

_____

_____

_____

_____

_____

_____

Dominant Negative Emotions. With the Fall, human beings became fearful and anxious. We also got to know shame and guilt. Depression and anger also entered the picture. List some of the negative emotions you struggle with:

_____

_____

_____

_____

_____

Too Many Choices. In the Garden of Eden, Adam and Eve could make a billion good choices and only one bad choice. They made that one bad choice (and you and I probably would have done the same thing!), and that means we're confronted every day with a ton of good and bad choices. List some of the countless decisions you face each day—and some of the bad choices you make:

_____

_____

_____

_____

_____

Attributes Become Needs. Another long-term effect of sin is that our three glowing strengths before the Fall became three glaring needs after the Fall. Acceptance was replaced by rejection, and so we have a need to belong. Innocence was replaced by guilt and shame, and so we need our self-worth to be restored. Authority was replaced by weakness and helplessness, and so we have a need for strength and self-control.

List some of the evidence you see in your life that you need to belong, that you fear rejection or that you know what peer pressure feels like:

_____

_____

_____

_____

_____

List some of the evidence you see that you have a poor self-image and need a sense of self-worth:

_____

_____

_____

_____

List some of the evidence you see that you want some control:

_____

_____

_____

_____

_____

Who's Meeting Your Needs? Sinful behavior is a wrong attempt to meet our basic needs. Are you allowing God to meet your needs or are you looking to the world to meet your needs? It's an issue of relationship and maturity. The better we understand our identity in Christ, the more we will grow in maturity. And the more mature we become, the easier it will be for us to choose what is right.

- What choices of what is right have become easier for you as you've become more mature as a person and/or as a Christian?

- What choices are still tough for you? Pray about those situations and, if you're brave, have a friend pray for you, too.

Your true identity is not based on what you do or what you have, but on who you are in Christ. After all, Jesus Christ came after Adam and won back for us the spiritual life Adam and Eve lost.

The triumph of Jesus and what it has gained for us is the theme of the next chapter.

START STOMPING!

Shout Down the World. Grab a bunch of magazines and cut out ads that tell you who you "should" be. Make a collage (that means glue them on a piece of paper) and then, with a Christian friend, consider the message. (The silliness of the message just might make you laugh.) Does what the world say you should be really matter in the big (eternal) scheme of things?

Say "Thanks!" Who has been there for you when you didn't feel you "belonged"? Does that person know you appreciate him or her? Send a note, give a flower, buy a piece of pizza at lunch—let that person know (in so many words or just by actions) that you appreciate the friendship!

Reach Out and Touch Someone. Where can you reach out and offer your friendship to someone who may need the sense of belonging that you've experienced? Pray aloud.

> *Okay, God, I see what I've inherited from Adam and Eve, and it's not pretty. You know, it's real hard to deal with being down on myself, with loneliness, with the inability to make good choices, with anger and depression and shame and guilt and fear. I don't want to hide from You or anyone else, but sometimes it's hard not to. God, help me hear Your truth. Help me really hear that You love me. And help me get to know You better. I pray in Jesus' name. Amen.*

STRENGTH GIVERS

These words are *for* you and *about* you. As you read each day's verse, ask yourself, "How would my life be different if I could live out this truth?"—and ask God to help you do so.

Monday:	Matthew 5:13
Tuesday:	Matthew 5:14
Wednesday:	Acts 1:8
Thursday:	John 15:16
Friday:	Ephesians 3:1

FOREVER DIFFERENT

Read the story of Tank and Turk and the Barbie twins, and then answer the following questions:

- Tank and Turk, those bundles of physical urges, sure behaved differently than Tank and Turk, the lean, mean, running machines. Why?

- Think about your perception of yourself. Are you more like Tank and Turk before the track coach discovered them or Tank and Turk after they started working out? Explain your answer.

Many Christians (and you may be one of them) are not enjoying the victory and freedom that is their inheritance in Christ because they have inaccurate ideas about themselves. If we don't know what God says about us and who we are in Christ, we will suffer from a poor self-image. We must get a handle on our true identity in Christ and lose our old identity in sinful Adam.

THE LIFE-CHANGING DIFFERENCE OF BEING IN CHRIST

Have you put your trust in Christ? Then, from God's perspective, you are no longer identified with Adam and his sin but with Jesus and His righteousness. Are you identifying with Him, though? Consider the following questions.

Unending Dependence on God. Adam depended on God to a point, but Jesus was completely dependent on God the Father.

- On a scale from Adam up to Jesus, evaluate your dependence on God. How well do you do in general?

- In what aspects of your life are you most independent on God? Why?

- What does the world—our society and your school campus—teach about dependence and independence? Which is acceptable in the world's eyes, and which is not? How does God figure into the world's message?

Uninterrupted Spiritual Life. Both Adam and Jesus were born spiritually alive. Adam died spiritually when he sinned, but Jesus never gave up His spiritual life because He never sinned. If you've accepted Christ as your Savior, you are no longer spiritually dead but alive in Him now and forever.

- Because of Adam, you were born spiritually dead, and sin continues to interfere with your Christian walk. What specific things tend to interrupt your spiritual life these days?

- What does it mean to you to pray, "Lead us not into temptation"?

- What can you learn about resisting temptation from Jesus in Matthew 4:1-11?

The differences between Adam and Jesus spell the difference between life and death for you and me. Read on!

WHAT A DIFFERENCE CHRIST'S DIFFERENCE MAKES IN US!

In 1 Corinthians 15:22, Paul writes, "As in Adam all die, so also in Christ all shall be made alive." Believers are "in Christ," and being in Christ is the most important part of our identity.

New Life Requires New Birth. We weren't born in Christ. We were born in sin (see Psalm 51:5). So what is God's plan for transforming us from being in Adam to being in Christ? His plan is for spiritual birth.

- What did you learn about your spiritual life in Christ from the comparison of physical birth to spiritual rebirth?

· You may have come across a couple mindblowers in the text. We're thinking of the statements "Eternal life is not something you get when you die" and "Salvation is not a future addition; it's a present transformation" (see John 17:3; 2 Corinthians 5:17). In plain English, what do these facts mean to you?

New Life Brings New Identity. Being a Christian is not just a matter of getting something; it's a matter of being someone. Being born again changed you into someone who didn't exist before. So what you get from God as His child isn't the point; it's who you are. And it's not what you do as a Christian that determines who you are; it's who you are that determines what you do. More mindblowers, right? Let's untangle them.

· If you think you're no good, you'll probably live like you're no good. Could this be your motto? In what ways are you living like you're no good?

· Do you see yourself as a child of God? Where in your life are you living in victory and freedom as Christ did?

· If you find yourself living as if you're no good more than you live according to the truth that you are a child of God, Satan may be one reason. What can you do to protect yourself from Satan's deception about your relationship to God and your value to Him? (We started your answer for you. That's just the kind of writers we are!)

1. <u>Read this book.</u>
2. <u>Do the "Start Stomping" activities.</u>
3. _____
4. _____
5. _____

New Life Results in a New Title. The Bible says we are saints because God calls us saints (see Ephesians 1:1; Philippians 1:1).

· What kind of person do you think of when you hear the word "saint"? Who comes to mind?

- What do you think about being called a saint yourself? How does that make you feel? How do you think God intends that title to make you feel?

- If you think of yourself as a sinner, how will you probably act? Give three or four examples from a typical day.

- As a child of God, you are a saint who unfortunately happens to sin, sometimes several times a day. But if you were to think of yourself as a saint, how would you act in some of the circumstances you just outlined?

You've heard it before and now you'll hear it again! What you do doesn't determine who you are; who you are determines what you do. Got that, saint?

WHAT IS TRUE OF CHRIST IS TRUE OF YOU

Yep, you read that right. What is true of Jesus now applies to you because you are in Christ. It's part of your identity.

Who Am I? Review the "Who Am I?" list that begins on page 26 of the text. (Some you will recognize from last chapter's "Strength Givers.") If you are in Christ, every one of these statements is completely true of you. They aren't true because of anything you've done. They're true because of what Jesus has done for you.

- Which one or two of these "Who Am I?" statements are the most encouraging to you today? Why?

- Which one or two of these "Who Am I?" statements are the most challenging to you today? Why?

- Which one or two of these "Who Am I?" statements are the hardest for you to believe? Why?

You can make all these traits more meaningful and productive in your life by simply choosing to believe what God has said about you. Believing what God says about you doesn't make it true. What God says about you is true, and therefore you believe it.

THE BRIGHT HOPE OF BEING A CHILD OF GOD

As the helpless and hopeless children of sinful Adam, there was nothing about us to make us acceptable to God. But through Jesus, God provided the only way for us to become part of His family. You are no longer a spiritual orphan; you are a child of God.

Special? Me? As a Christian, you are someone very special.

> • Who did what to give you that special status?

> • Read 1 John 3:1-3. What hope do you find in this description of God's love and its effect on your life?

We are children of God—now! When we believe that, we begin to live like the children of God we are. But we must see ourselves as children of God in order to live like children of God.

VIP Invite. Just in case you weren't ready to accept the invitation earlier, we'll extend it again. Would you like to become a child of God? Are you ready to receive Jesus into your life (see John 1:12)? Let God know of your choice by saying the following prayer:

> *Lord Jesus, I need You. Thank You for dying on the cross for my sins. I believe that You were resurrected from the dead in order that I might have spiritual life. I put my trust for eternal life in You and invite You into my life to be my Lord and Master. I no longer want to live independently of You. Thank You for giving me eternal life. In Jesus' name I pray. Amen.*

START STOMPING!

Celebrate Dependence Day! In the Old Testament, God's people would build altars to remind them of God's faithfulness. With some small stones, build an altar. (Or, if you prefer, draw a picture.) Then on an index card write down the instance(s) of God's faithfulness this altar is commemorating. As you dedicate this altar, ask God to forgive your independence and to teach you greater dependence on Him.

Poster Time. Get a piece of poster board and then get creative! Use marking pens, pictures from magazines, Bible references, Christian symbols and old photographs to do whatever it takes to illustrate and get into your brain the truth: "What I do doesn't determine who I am; who I am determines what I do—and I am a child of God!"

Ears to Hear. Just in case you didn't do what the text strongly encouraged you to do, we'll invite you once again to read aloud the "Who Am I?" list. Yep—out loud! And stick your name into those statements, too, for greater impact ("I, Poindexter, am a child of God." "I, Esmerelda, am a new person. My past is forgiven and everything is new.")

> *God, it's hard to get my mind around all You've done for me. Through the death of Your Son, Jesus, You've made it possible for me to be Your child. All I have to do is accept Your invitation. Thank You for helping me hear and respond to that invitation. Now, God, please help me learn how to live as Your child. I pray in Jesus' name. Amen.*

STRENGTH GIVERS

These words are for you and about you. As you read each day's verse, ask yourself, "How would my life be different if I could live out this truth?"—and ask God to help you do so.

Monday:	1 Corinthians 1:30
Tuesday:	John 1:12
Wednesday:	2 Corinthians 5:17
Thursday:	Ephesians 1:1
Friday:	1 Peter 2:9-10

SEE YOURSELF FOR WHO YOU REALLY ARE

Read the opening story about Claire and then answer the following questions:

- What does my (Neil's) account of Claire teach you?

- What was Claire's "secret"?

- Claire accepted herself for who God said she was in Christ—His child. She also confidently committed herself to God's main goal for her life—to be like Christ and to love people. Can you say the same about yourself?

- What keeps you from being more like Claire?

Our guess is that, like most Christians and unlike Claire, you struggle to accept who you are. You don't simply accept yourself as a child of God. We'd also guess that, unlike Claire, you find it hard to be focused primarily on God's call to be like Christ and love other people. Claire's experience reminds us how important it is to base our Christian lives on what we believe instead of how we behave. We need a firm grip on what God says about who we are before we will experience much success at living the Christian life.

BELIEF BEFORE BEHAVIOR

A healthy Christian lifestyle is the result of a healthy Christian belief system, not the other way around. If what we believe about God and ourselves is shaky, then our day-to-day behavior will be shaky.

Get a Grip on God's Grace. "Grace" is one of those words you may have heard a lot but no one's ever really defined, and you've never asked because you felt you should already know what it means! Well, a classic definition of "grace" is "unmerited favor." Grace is goodness we receive that we don't deserve and couldn't earn. It's God's gift of forgiveness and eternal life through the death of His Son, Jesus.

- Remember Myndee Hudson? What about her story hit you the hardest? Be specific.

- What has happened in your life to help you realize what's really important?

- To quote Myndee, "When you know you're going to die, you only care about things that are going to last. Before I was sick, Jesus was only a part of my life. Now He's everything to me." Is Jesus only a part of your life? Or is He everything to you?

- What do your answers tell you about yourself and how you're living life?

Getting right with God means settling once and for all the issue that God is your loving Father. You are a child of God, you are created in His image, and you have been declared righteous by Him because you have put your trust in Christ.

- When you shift your focus away from your identity as God's child and try to be something you're not or wish you were someone else, you'll struggle. What interferes with your focus on the truth that you are God's child?

- Read again these powerful truths: We don't serve God to gain His acceptance; we are accepted, so we serve God. We don't follow Him in order to be loved; we are loved, so we follow Him. What are you doing to earn God's acceptance?

- What are you doing to earn His love?

Make your answers to the two previous questions the topic of a prayer. Ask God to remove the barriers to your belief that you are His child. Ask Him to free you from feeling you have to earn His acceptance and love. And ask Him to protect you from Satan's efforts to convince you that you are unworthy and will always be unacceptable to God. Remember—you are a saint whom God has declared righteous. Believing this truth about your identity will set you free.

The Fallout from God's Grace. God's grace has far-reaching effects on our lives, as the list of truths that begins on page 34 suggests. Review this list and then answer the following questions:

- Which one or two of these "Since I Am in Christ" statements are the most encouraging to you today? Why?

- Which one or two of these "Since I Am in Christ" statements are the most challenging to you today? Why?

- Which one or two of these "Since I Am in Christ" statements are the hardest for you to believe? Why?

Understanding who you are in Christ won't change the circumstances of your life. But your perception of your identity makes a big difference in your success at dealing with the challenges and conflicts that come your way.

THERE'S A DIFFERENCE

You are a child of God—period. There's absolutely nothing you can do to make yourself more a child of God. But you can enjoy a more harmonious relationship with God if you diligently try to obey Him.

- What can you do to change your relationship with your heavenly Father? (Yes, this is a trick question.)

- What can you do to affect how well you get along with your heavenly Father? Think about your relationship to your earthly father or to my (Neil's) relationship to my father.

BELIEVE WHAT YOU PERCEIVE IN OTHERS

As important as it is for you to believe in your true identity as a child of God, it is equally important that you see other Christians for who they are and treat them the way they should be treated. Gulp!

- Okay, who in the course of your week could you have treated more like the child of God that they are?

- What did the story of Miss Thompson and Teddy teach you about how we are to treat other people?

- Write out Ephesians 4:29. When you blew it, who has given you grace through his or her words? Who has loved you no matter what you did or didn't do?

- Who can you, a new recruit for God's construction crew, build up through your words today? Do it!

BELIEVING THE TRUTH ABOUT YOURSELF

Remember Jenny? At what stage of Jenny's transformation are you right now? Are you . . .

- Depressed, wondering where to turn?

- Waiting for someone to affirm your value to God?

- Beginning to understand that you are a child of God, no better and no worse than any other of His children?

- Walking by faith, seeing yourself for who you really are in Christ?

- Wherever you see yourself along this time line from Jenny's life, think about where you want to be. What goals do you have for your walk of faith? Choose one goal and identify the next step you will take toward reaching that goal. Now take that step!

You are a righteous and accepted child of God—and that is solid truth from the Bible. Read and reread the identity statements listed in the second and third chapters of this book. See yourself in them. Believe them. Walk in them. As you walk by faith, your behavior as a Christian will begin to conform to what you believe.

START STOMPING!

This Test Could Change Your Life. Take the test that I (Dave) challenged Kristy to take, and see what happens. Read aloud the "Since I Am in Christ" statements and really listen to what God is saying to you about you.

Tune-Up Time! How harmonious is your relationship with God right now? Disobedience means disharmony. Where are you being disobedient? Fess up! Receive forgiveness! Enjoy harmony with God.

Find a Friend. Living a Christian life isn't easy, so don't try to do it alone. Find a friend—someone who knows the Lord and has walked closely with Him for a good while—and let this person know where you're at and what you need. Do you need affirmation and encouragement like Jenny did? Do you struggle to believe you're valuable to God? Do you need help obeying God's commands in a certain area of your life? Do you need prayer? Let this person give you the support you need. Give him or her the opportunity to be an active member of God's construction crew.

> *God, I feel like the father who wanted Jesus to heal his sick boy (see Mark 9:14-27). Like that dad who believed You could heal his son, I believe You can help me. But also like that dad who said, "If you can do anything . . ." I need help with my unbelief. I believe, God, that I am Your child. Help my unbelief. Amen.*

STRENGTH GIVERS

These words are *for* you and *about* you. As you read each day's verse, ask yourself, "How would my life be different if I could live out this truth?"—and ask God to help you do so.

Monday:	1 Corinthians 6:19-20
Tuesday:	2 Corinthians 5:21
Wednesday:	Ephesians 1:4
Thursday:	Ephesians 1:7-8
Friday:	Romans 5:1

Something Old, Something New

What's the difference between being a saint who sins rather than being a sinner? It's more than just playing with words. Our position in Christ is settled and solid, but our daily actions, often marked by failures and disobedience, disturb the harmony of our relationships with God.

- Read Romans 7:19,24. What good do you want to do that you can't seem to do?

- What wrong that you don't want to do, do you find yourself doing anyway?

Your answer to the preceding question points to the biggest problem for us Christians—the sinful side of our sainthood. The more we understand about our old sinful selves, our new selves in Christ and the sin we can't seem to shake, the better prepared we will be to grow in our identity in Christ.

FROM SINNER TO SAINT

First review the truth. What do the following verses say about you who have accepted Jesus as your Lord and Savior?

- Romans 8:9
- 2 Corinthians 5:17
- Ephesians 5:8
- Colossians 1:13

We have changed kingdoms: We are members of God's kingdom, not Satan's. When we first trusted Christ, the darkness departed and we are now light. We are not partly new and partly old with two creatures inside battling for supremacy. But still we struggle with Satan's temptations, darkness and the old self . . .

- Remember the story of Eustace in C. S. Lewis's *Voyage of the Dawn Treader*? What does Eustace's transformation tell you about your change from sinner to saint?

If you believe you are part dragon and part human, you will live an unfruitful life. When God took away your sin, He cut away your dragon skin (and dragon heart) and you became a totally new creature. Learning to think and act like a new creature in Christ (the outer change called "sanctification") continues throughout life. But learning to live successfully like a new creature will only happen when you accept the truth that you already are a new creature.

The Nature of the Matter. Before you came to Christ, you were dead in sin, subject to Satan's power, and living completely to fulfill sinful lusts and desires (see Ephesians 2:1-3). When you came into relationship with God through your new birth, you didn't add a new divine nature to your old sinful nature. You exchanged natures (see 2 Corinthians 5:17).

- What evidence do you see in your life and in your heart that you have indeed exchanged natures? Where have you had glimpses of your new divine nature?

- Why is having that new divine nature essential to being able to grow in your relationship with the Lord and become more Christlike?

Either One or the Other. Ephesians 5:8 states, "You were formerly darkness, but now you are light in the Lord; walk as children of light."

- What's the difference between being darkness and being in darkness? What does this tell you about yourself before you knew Jesus?

- What's the difference between being light and being in light? What does this tell you, a believer, about your role in the world?

• What instruction follows the statement that you are light—and what does that command mean in terms of your everyday life?

In the coming chapters, we'll look more closely at what it means to walk by faith and walk in the Spirit. Right now, though, consider how crucial it is that you have the nature of Christ in you.

With Christ's nature within, you can be more like Christ, not just act like Him. In what areas of your life today do you most need to be like Christ, not just act like Him? Let God know that's where you need His transforming touch.

God knows we can't measure up to His standards on our own, so He gives us an entirely new self—the life of Christ in us. This astounding act of grace enables us to become the people God wants us to be.

IS THE "OLD MAN" ALIVE, DYING OR ALREADY DEAD?

Before we came to Christ, we were sinners because it was our natures—our old selves, our "natural" ways—to sin. We couldn't accept or understand the things of the Spirit.

Rest in Peace. At salvation, your old inner self died by crucifixion with Christ (see Romans 6:6; Galatians 2:20).

• Your old self (the sinner) and your old nature (sinfulness) died with Christ on the cross and are gone forever. Does that mean you are now sinless? Support your answer with specific evidence from your life.

Sin and Satan are still around, and they are strong and appealing. But because of the crucifixion of the old self, sin's power over us is broken. We are no longer under any obligation to serve sin, to obey sin or to respond to sin.

• We sin when we make a willful decision to allow ourselves to act independently of God (which is how our old self acted all the time!). What decisions from the past seven days came to mind as you read that definition of sin? Let God know you're aware of those decisions to act independently of Him and ask His forgiveness (see 1 John 1:9).

When we make the wrong decision to act independently of God, we violate our new natures and our new identity. Such actions must be confessed and turned away from.

Once Dead, Always Dead. Colossians 3:3 begins with the words "for you have died." Paul is describing what has happened, not telling you something you need to do.

- Where, if at all, are you—like the pastor who visited me (Neil)—struggling to let your old self die?

- God expects you to know, accept and believe that your old self has died and been replaced by a new self, controlled by a new nature. What freedom comes with accepting this truth?

The new life that characterizes your new self is nothing less than the life of Jesus Christ implanted in you. The old self is dead, once and for all.

WHERE DOES THE FLESH FIT INTO THE PICTURE?

As my (Neil's) Navy experience reflects, when we're programmed to react a certain way under one skipper's authority, it takes time to get used to a new skipper. Yep, we're talking about the old self who operated under the authority of sin (the old skipper) and the new self who is in Christ (your new skipper).

Reacting to Your Old Skipper. Our old sinful selves with their sinful natures were cruel, self-serving skippers under the authority of Satan himself. By God's grace, we have a new admiral—Jesus—and a new skipper: Our new selves are powered by the divine nature of Jesus Christ. So why do we live as if our old skippers are still in control? Because everything we learned before we became Christians was programmed into our brains.

- What habits and patterns of thinking that you learned from the world still influence how you act?

- In what areas of your life do you especially tend to operate independently of God and center your interests on yourself?

When you were born again, your old self died and your new self came to life. But your flesh (your previously learned independence) remained. So even though your old skipper is gone, your flesh remains in opposition to God as a programmed tendency for sin—living independently of God.

Responding to Your New Skipper. As a Christian you are no longer "in the flesh" or spiritually dead. You are in Christ. But even though you are not in the flesh, you may still choose to walk according to the flesh (see Romans 8:12-13). You may still act independently of God by saying yes to the patterns and habits programmed into your mind by the world you lived in.

- It's your responsibility to keep the flesh and its deeds from dominating your life. How well are you doing that? If you're experiencing success, what's your secret? If you're struggling, try to figure out why.

How can you keep the flesh from dominating your life? First, by learning to walk in the Spirit (see Galatians 5:1) and, second, by letting God transform your pattern of thinking by "the renewing of your mind" (Romans 12:2). Those two topics are the focus of the next five chapters. (Yes, five! This is important stuff!) But first, a few more things about sin and sainthood.

WHAT ROLE DOES SIN PLAY IN OUR STRUGGLE TOWARD SAINTLY BEHAVIOR?

When you received Christ, the power of sin to dominate you was broken. You no longer have to sin, but sin still strongly appeals to your flesh, tempting you to act independently of God. It is your responsibility to not let sin reign in your life (see Romans 6:12-13).

Doing What I Don't Want to Do. We're back to recognizing once again, with Paul, that we know what we should be doing, but we can't do it (see Romans 7:15-16).

- According to Romans 7:20, why can't you and I do what we know we should be doing?

• What did you learn about yourself and the sin living in you from the comparison of sin to a sliver in your finger (see page 51)?

On the Battleground. Now let's look at where the struggle to do what you want to do takes place.

• According to Romans 7:22-23, where does your desire to do what's right come from?

• Where does sin attack in an attempt to keep you from doing right?

• Where do these opponents—your new self and your flesh—wage war?

• What kind of defensive strategy does that location suggest to you?

The battleground between your new self (your inner being) and your flesh (your previously learned independence) is your mind. That's why it is so important for you to learn how to renew your mind (see Romans 12:2) and take every thought captive to the obedience of Christ (see 2 Corinthians 10:5). So stay tuned—and remember that, thanks to God, the battle for your mind is a winnable war.

START STOMPING!

A Little Help from a Friend. Sometimes we are the last to notice any changes or growth in ourselves because we live with ourselves day in and day out. It may be hard for you to identify any changes in your life and in your heart since you named Jesus your Lord and exchanged natures. So ask a friend or two what changes they have seen and are seeing in you as you continue along your Christian walk.

Bon Voyage, Skipper. Get together with a close friend or two from church and have a farewell party for the old skipper. That means good food and plenty of it as you talk about the old skipper and celebrate his or her departure. Share your lists of those habits and patterns of thinking that each of you learned from the world and that still influence how you act. Let each other know those areas of your life where you tend to operate independently of God and center your interests on yourself. Then, as a way of saying farewell to these things, agree to ask each other from time to time how life under the new skipper is. This will remind you that the old skipper is in fact gone and encourage you to respond only to the new skipper.

Drive Defensively! Okay, the opponents have been identified and the battleground located. The war between your new self (your inner being) and your flesh (your previously learned independence) occurs in your mind. Before we get to the five chapters on how to win the war, ask some Christian friends (ideally, some folks who've been dealing with this battle for a lot longer than you have) what they do to stand strong in the Lord and resist the appeals of the flesh, their old skippers. No need to wait until the next chapter to start driving defensively!

> *God, I could have written those words that Paul said—I do what I don't want to do and I don't do what I want to do. And sometimes it's awfully easy to act independently of You. I had a lot of practice doing that! I'm glad this chapter reminded me that this struggle against independence and sin is a winnable war. I'm sure anxious to learn how to win. Help me stand strong in You against the appeal of sin, that old skipper I know too well. Thanks. I pray in Jesus' name. Amen.*

STRENGTH GIVERS

These words are *for* you and *about* you! As you read each day's verse, ask yourself, "How would my life be different if I could live out this truth?"—and ask God to help you do so.

Monday:	Romans 6:1-6
Tuesday:	1 Thessalonians 5:5
Wednesday:	Galatians 2:20
Thursday:	1 Corinthians 3:16
Friday:	1 John 3:1-2

BECOMING THE SPIRITUAL PERSON YOU WANT TO BE

Think of someone in whom you see Christ. Why does that person come to mind? What about that person reminds you of Christ?

- I (Dave) received the compliment of a lifetime when the Kenyan soldiers told their commander they saw Christ in me. What does it take to be a Christian in whom others can see Christ daily?

- What will move us away from selfishness and fleshly desires to loving service to God and others?

- Any ideas at this point?

If people are to see Christ in our lives, we first need a firm grip on our identity in Christ We need to accept the reality that, since we are in Christ, His divine nature is part of us. Second, we must begin to renew our minds and retrain the flesh. This living out our true identity in Christ is called walking in the Spirit. Let's look at some of Scripture's guidelines for doing so.

THREE PERSONS AND THE SPIRIT

In 1 Corinthians 2:14–3:3, Paul talks about three kinds of people: (1) the natural person, (2) the spiritual person, and (3) the fleshly person. Let's look at each closely.

The Natural Person. The natural person is spiritually dead, separated from God, living independently from God. The natural person can't help but sin.

- Review the description of the natural person and the accompanying chart. Where do you see your old self under the old skipper?

- List some of the specific changes in your body, emotions, will, mind and purpose since you named Jesus as Lord. What have you left behind? What don't you struggle with as much anymore? Thank God for His transforming work in your life.

The Spiritual Person. The spiritual person has been transformed. When he accepted Christ, his spirit was united with God's Spirit. He now enjoys forgiveness of sin, acceptance in God's family and the knowledge that he is worth something.

- How did you react to the description of the spiritual person?

- Was it encouraging? Discouraging? Both? Why?

List some of the specific characteristics of body, emotions, will, mind and purpose that you want God to bring about in you. Ask Him to show you how to cooperate with Him in His transforming work so that you can become more mature in Christ and make better choices more consistently.

The Fleshly Person. The fleshly person is a Christian—spiritually alive in Christ and declared righteous by God—but that's where the similarity ends. Instead of being directed and controlled by the Spirit, this believer chooses to follow the temptations of his flesh.

- Where, if at all, do you unfortunately see yourself in the description of the fleshly person?

- Why do so many of us believers live so far below our potential in Christ?

- Many of us forget who we are in Christ, so we don't actively apply that truth to our daily walks. Also, we don't realize how much Satan tries to block our growth and maturity as God's children. Which of these reasons—and maybe some others as well—contribute to your tendencies to be a fleshly person? Confess those aloud to God and ask for His help.

GUIDELINES FOR THE SPIRIT-FILLED WALK

Know at the start that there isn't any magic formula for walking in the Spirit. Walking according to the Spirit is more like a relationship with a good friend than a list of dos and don'ts.

What the Spirit-filled Walk Is Not. The Spirit-filled walk is neither license (totally disregarding God's loving guidelines and doing whatever you want) nor legalism (obeying a bunch of dos and don'ts). Being led by the Spirit means you are free to do the right thing and to live a responsible life.

- First, consider the results of license. When have you learned from experience that God's loving guidelines exist to protect you?

- Asked differently, when have you made a poor decision and been in bondage to the consequences of your choice?

God's laws are designed to protect you, not tie you down and strangle you. Your real freedom is your ability to choose to live obediently within the protective guidelines God has given.

- Now think about legalism. When has your response to someone laying down the law been the immediate desire to cross that line and perhaps actually crossing it?

- When it comes to a Spirit-filled walk, demanding good things (Bible study, prayer, regular church attendance and witnessing) is no more effective than forbidding bad things. What's happened when you've approached these good things as "shoulds" or "have tos" rather than as the means to a closer relationship to Jesus?

God's law—those rules for behavior we find in the Bible—is a necessary, protective standard and guideline. When we live within that law, we are free to develop a spirit-to-Spirit relationship with God (see 1 Corinthians 6:17; 2 Corinthians 3:5-6).

What the Spirit-filled Walk Is. Again, the Spirit-filled walk is neither license nor legalism but liberty. It's the freedom to be who we already are in Christ: loved and accepted children of God. And our freedom in Christ is freedom to choose whether to walk according to the Spirit or according to the flesh.

- Why is it key that we are to walk in the Spirit and not sit?

- Why is it key that we are to walk in the Spirit and not run? What does the action of walking as opposed to sitting or running suggest to you?

We are to walk, not be sitting in idle and letting our mind coast in neutral. And we are to walk, not be running in an effort to achieve the Spirit-filled life through endless, exhausting activity.

- When are you tempted to sit back and not move?

- In what circumstances do you tend to run ahead and try to achieve the Spirit-filled life through lots of activity?

- Read Matthew 11:28-30. In your own words, explain what this image says about the Spirit-filled life, its pace and how to live it. Comment, too, on what this image says about how God chooses to get things done in the world.

The yoke that Jesus offers means a restful walk with Him. And that picture of walking in the Spirit with Jesus points out that God has chosen to work in partnership with you to do His work in the world today. As remarkable as it sounds, neither Jesus nor you will accomplish much unless both of you pull your side of the yoke.

Walking by Being Led. Walking according to the Spirit is also a matter of being led by the Spirit (see Romans 8:14). Consider the following two-part truth and what it means for you.

- "God won't make you walk in the Spirit." What does this statement say to you about your freedom and your responsibility as a child of God?

- "The devil can't make you walk in the flesh." What does this statement say to you about your freedom of choice and your ability to stand strong against Satan's efforts to draw you away from God?

The Spirit-filled walk is one of being led, not driven, and it is your choice to follow either the leading of the Spirit or the desires of the flesh.

The Proof Is in the Fruit. How can you know if you're being led by the Spirit or the flesh? By looking at your behavior, and Galatians 5 gives us some standards by which we can evaluate our attitudes and actions.

- Read Galatians 5:19-21. What kinds of attitudes and be- haviors suggest a person is walking according to the flesh?

- Read Galatians 5:22-23. What kinds of attitudes and be- haviors suggest a person is following the Spirit's leading?

Walking according to the Spirit is a moment-by-moment, day-by- day experience. When you step off the path of the Spirit, confess and renounce your sin to God and anyone you may have offended, receive forgiveness, and return to the right path.

- To whom do you need to confess when you've made a wrong choice?

- How does confession model and even encourage growth?

In Christ, you are free from the power of sin. But if Satan can con- vince you that you're not free, you'll remain in captivity. The more you walk in step with Jesus, the better prepared you'll be to recog- nize Satan's deception and disarm his strategy.

START STOMPING!

Grab Those Scissors! It's time to be creative! Make a collage, a draw- ing or a poster that will remind you of what a Spirit-filled walk is and maybe even isn't. Illustrate the truth of Matthew 11:28-30. Draw a slash through those words and/or pictures that communi- cate what the Spririt-filled walk is not. Make it a powerful encour- agement to live the kind of life you want to be living.

Yep, It's a Step of Faith. Find a blindfold and a friend. Cover your eyes with the blindfold and have your friend lead you around for five minutes. Pay attention to what you're thinking and feeling as you walk along. After five minutes, switch roles. Now as you lead your blindfolded friend along, notice again your thoughts and feelings. What does this exercise teach you about walking the Spirit-filled walk? What do being led and leading help you understand about God, the One who wants to lead you?

Get Those Hands Dirty. There's something awesome about watching something grow—and there's also much to be learned. So plant something—a single seed, a row of vegetables, a tiny plant. As you work to keep it growing, think of yourself as the seed and God as your gardener and let your little plant encourage you in your own growth in the Lord. He's doing the work for your growth. Like your little plant, you just need to receive all He wants to give you that will help you grow in Him.

> *God, I get uncomfortable looking at the kind of person You want me to be and realizing the kind of person I usually am. That description of the spiritual person seems pretty unreachable, and the description of the fleshly person sure makes me squirm. I'm glad You give me guidelines for how to live the kind of life I want to live for You. It helped me to see that walking with You isn't license or legalism. Help me get to know Your voice better so that I can recognize it easily, and give me the strength I need to make the right choice to follow Your Spirit's leading and not the desires of the flesh. Amen.*

STRENGTH GIVERS

These words are *for* you and *about* you! As you read each day's verse, ask yourself, "How would my life be different if I could live this truth?"—and ask God to help you do so.

Monday:	1 Corinthians 2:16
Tuesday:	1 John 5:18
Wednesday:	Colossians 1:14
Thursday:	Colossians 1:27
Friday:	2 Timothy 1:7

THE POWER OF POSITIVE BELIEVING

The adventure film *Indiana Jones and the Last Crusade* offers us a poor picture of faith as Indy steps off a ledge for what appeared to be a long deadly fall. Instead, after only a few feet, he lands on a pathway of stone, unseen from the ledge above.

- What adventure scene would you use as a picture of faith? Be as specific as possible.

- Faith—believing who God is, what He says and what He does—is vital to the Christian life. It is central to everything we do as Christians—to our daily living, to our spiritual growth and to growing up in Christ. Is believing in God the same as Indiana Jones's blind leap into nothingness? Explain why you answered yes or no.

- Unlike the riddle makers who choreographed Indy's adventure, God doesn't demand blind faith. He doesn't require that we believe in Him without any evidence at all. How has God shown you—in general as one of His people as well as in very personal ways—that He is worthy of your trust?

Jesus became a man and lived among us, and God's prophets spoke specifically about the Messiah who would come. Our faith is firmly based on the solid evidence of the life of Jesus Christ and the truth of God's Word. We didn't have to jump into a bottomless chasm when we named Him Lord and Savior.

THE DIMENSIONS OF DOWN-TO-EARTH FAITH

Now let's work on bringing faith out of the mystical realm of the spiritual and into the practical, nuts-and-bolts area of everyday living.

Faith Depends on Its Object. Faith is not simply a matter of believing. It's what we believe and who we believe in that determines whether or not our faith will be rewarded.

- What are some of the things you put faith in every day? Start your list by thinking about who you're trusting when, for instance, you ride in a car or grab a burger at the local drive-thru.

- What happens when the object of your faith fails you? How do you feel? What do you think? What happens to your faith? Give several different examples.

- How is faith in Jesus different from faith in the objects and people you listed above?

Jesus Christ is the ultimate faith object. The fact that He never changes makes Him totally trustworthy (see Numbers 23:19; Malachi 3:6; 13:8). He has never failed to do all that He said He would do or be all that He said He would be. He is eternally faithful.

The Depth of Faith Is Determined by the Depth of Your Knowledge of the Object. We struggle with our faith in God when our knowledge of Him is insufficient. Faith in God only fails when we misunderstand God and His ways.

- As you look back on a time when you struggled with your faith in God, what didn't you understand about Him?

- What did you learn about God through that experience?

- If you want your faith in God to grow, you must increase your understanding of Him. What are you doing to keep growing in your understanding of God?

The only limit to our faith is our knowledge and understanding of God. That knowledge grows every time we read the Bible, memorize a Scripture verse, participate in a Bible study or meditate on a biblical truth. The potential for your faith to grow as you seek to know God is boundless.

Faith Is an Action Word. Faith isn't just saying, "I believe." Faith without action is not faith (see James 2:17-18). Faith involves action. Faith makes a move. Faith speaks up.

- Evaluate your faith. Are you a spiritual couch potato or an active-duty soldier following Jesus' directions? Are you sometimes one and sometimes the other? If so, why? What keeps you stretched out on the couch sometimes (or always)?

- Now think about your participation in church or youth group. Are you treating it like an infirmary or a military outpost? Why?

- God's people—the Church—exist to be change agents in the world. What are you doing to be actively involved in God's cause? (Such activity is crucial to a real faith.) What could you be doing to be more actively involved in God's cause?

"If You Believe You Can, You Can." Okay, you're not much into poetry, but read the poem on page 70 one more time anyway.

- When have you seen one or two of the truths of this poem acted out in real life, preferably your life? Be specific.

- How is positive believing different from positive thinking?

Positive believing is as valid as the object of faith, which is the living and written Word of God—Jesus Christ and the Bible. With the all-powerful God of the universe as the object of your Christian faith, there's hardly any limit to the spiritual heights that your positive believing can take you.

Twenty Cans of Success. Someone has said that success comes in cans and failure in cannots. The "Twenty Cans of Success" will help expand your knowledge of Almighty God and build your faith.

- Read through the "Twenty Cans of Success" again. Which can holds a truth that has helped you in the past? Describe the situation and how that truth was illustrated.

• Think about what's going on in your life right now. Which can do you need to open today? Let that particular truth shape a quick prayer to God!

The quicksand of cannots is not where believers need to dwell, and the "Twenty Cans of Success" will help you climb out of the mire. Open one or more whenever you need them!

WHAT HAPPENS WHEN I STUMBLE IN MY WALK OF FAITH?

Have you ever felt, after an especially extreme stumble and fall, that God is ready to give up on you? Do you ever fear that you've crossed the line and moved beyond the limits of God's love? Then keep reading! These truths are for you!

God Loves You Just the Way You Are. God's love is not based on what you do or don't do. Read that sentence again: God's love is not based on what you do or don't do.

• What did you learn about God's love from Mandy's discussion with me (Neil)?

• Where in your life have you felt that being loved and accepted is based on what you do or don't do?

God is different from those situations and people you just identified. God loves you not because you are lovable but because it is His nature to love you. God loves you because God is love. And why not read that again, too? Say it aloud: "God loves me not because I am lovable but because it is His nature to love me. God loves me because God is love."

God Loves You No Matter What You Do. God wants us to do good, of course. But, through His Son, Jesus, God has already made provision for our failures so that His love continues constant in spite of what we do.

• When have you been able to keep loving someone despite something hurtful he or she did?

- What did this situation teach you about how God loves you?

- When has someone kept on loving you despite something awful, wrong or insensitive you did?

- What did this situation show you about how God loves you?

God will keep on loving you no matter what you've done. No matter what you do or how you fail, God has no desire not to love you and accept you completely. Even when you forget who you are as His child and stumble off the path of the Spirit-led life, He still loves you. Again, God loves you simply because it is His nature to love.

START STOMPING!

Get Real! God's people—the Church—exist to be change agents in the world, taking a stand, living by faith and accomplishing something for God. (Yes, you've read those words before, but they're worth repeating.) Genuine faith is active faith, so let's get real! Come up with a project that you and a friend, or you and some members of your church youth group, could do to walk your talk in your community. Is there a soup kitchen you could volunteer at? Do some older folks you know need help with yard work or home and car repairs? Does your church need volunteers in the nursery? Look around for projects that you can do, and then go accomplish something for God!

You Can Do It! Get a couple of good-sized pieces of paper (and we don't mean wimpy 8.5 x 11-inch sheets) and cut out two soup cans. Okay. Next step. Earlier you identified a can that has worked for you and a can that you need right now. Write out in your own words, on one of your paper cans, the can that helped. On the other can, write out the can you need. Take the can that worked to a friend or, better yet, to youth group and be ready to share your story and ready to learn from other people's stories. Now you can do one of two things with the can that describes what you need. If you're up to it, share it with someone or several people who will pray for you. If that's just too risky—and it's okay if it is—put your can somewhere that you'll see often so that you'll get that truth drilled into your brain and will start living the can.

Snip! Snip! Snip! Or an Exercise in (God's) Forgivenes. Maybe a pair
of scissors will help you understand what God has done for you
and drive home the truth that God loves you just the way you
are, no matter what you've done. Cut some 8.5 x 11-inch paper
into 8, 10 or 12 smaller pieces (depending on how big you write).
On each of these smaller pieces of paper, write one of the ways
you've failed to be the person you know God wants you to be.
Write down all the sins you struggle to forgive yourself for. Write
down all the ways you've blown it—big time and not so big time.
When you've finished, let each one be a brief prayer of confession
and renunciation. Then cut the piece of paper into the tiniest
pieces possible and throw them away. That sin is gone, forgiven
by God completely and forever. Okay? He will never hold them
against you. Okay!

> *Your love really is pretty amazing, God. You'll love me just the way
> I am and no matter what I do. That's a pretty good deal for me,
> and yet sometimes I ignore Your love and do what I want to do
> instead of what You want me to do. I'm sorry, God. Please forgive
> me. And please help me learn to trust You more. I need to open
> those "cans of success" and get to know You better. And, knowing
> You, I want to get out there and accomplish something for You.
> Show me what You want me to do and then be with me as I do it. I
> pray in Jesus' name. Amen.*

STRENGTH GIVERS

These words are *for* you and *about* you! As you read each day's
verse, ask yourself, "How would my life be different if I could live
out this truth?"—and ask God to help you do so.

Monday:	Colossians 3:12
Tuesday:	Ephesians 2:10
Wednesday:	Romans 8:31
Thursday:	1 Peter 5:7
Friday:	John 16:33

YOU CAN'T LIVE BEYOND WHAT YOU BELIEVE

You've probably never thought about how much your faith is like driving a golf ball off a tee. But if your faith is off, your walk will be off. If your walk is off, you can be sure it's because you faith is off. And the longer you hold on to a poor belief system, the more "off" your walk will be. So let's take a look at your belief system.

Belief Quiz—Parts One and Two. If you haven't already, take the two-part Belief Quiz.

- What surprised you about the questions on the Belief Quiz? What kind of questions did you expect?

- Why is it important to look at what you believe will bring you success, significance, fulfillment, satisfaction, happiness, fun, security and peace?

If what you believe about these eight values—success, significance, fulfillment, satisfaction, happiness, fun, security and peace—doesn't line up with what God says about them, your walk of faith will be off to the same degree that your belief is off. Keep that in mind as you work through this chapter and the next.

FEELINGS ARE GOD'S RED FLAG OF WARNING

God desires His children to experience success, significance, fulfillment, satisfaction, happiness, fun, security and peace. But sometimes our ideas about how to achieve these goals are not completely in harmony with God's plans and goals for us, and God can use our emotions to let us know that we may be holding on to a poor goal based on a wrong belief.

Anger Signals a Blocked Goal. When we feel angry about a relationship or a project, it's usually because someone or something has blocked our goal.

  • When has anger signaled a blocked goal for you?

Anxiety Signals an Uncertain Goal. When we feel anxious (worried and afraid at the same time), our anxiety may be signaling our uncertainty about the goal we have chosen.

  • When has anxiety helped you recognize your uncertainty about a goal you had set for yourself?

Depression Signals an Impossible Goal. Depression is a signal that our goal, no matter how spiritual or noble, may never be reached. Depression is the expression of hopelessness.

  • When has depression signaled that you are working toward a goal you have little or no chance of achieving?

  • Depression resulting from an impossible goal can also be related to a wrong concept of God. What was David's wrong concept of God in Psalm 13?

  • What did David do to get out of his depression? What truth did he begin to focus on?

If Satan can destroy your belief in God, you will lose your source of hope. But if you can follow David's example and move away from your wrong concept of God to the truth about Him, you will once again find hope.

Wrong Responses to Those Who Frustrate Goals. When our happiness or success hinges on reaching a goal that can be blocked or that is uncertain or impossible, we may attempt to control or manipulate the people and circumstances that stand between us and success.

  • How do you tend to respond to people who block your goals? Do you get bitter, angry or resentful? Do you feel sorry for yourself? Do you take charge and become a manipulation master as Darcy did?

• Which of the answers to the preceding questions are pleasing to God?

Bad goals can mean bad situations between friends. Unless we adjust our goals, we'll waste months and possibly years living in bitter defeat, hardly the victorious lives God would have us live.

HOW CAN I TURN BAD GOALS INTO GOOD GOALS?

What's a "Good Goal"? Good question. Let's take a moment and define a good goal.

• In light of what you've just learned about goals from the discussion of anger, anxiety and depression, how would you define a good goal?

If God has a goal for your life, it cannot be blocked; its fulfillment is neither uncertain nor impossible. A good goal, then, is God's goal for you.

• What was God's goal for a young woman named Mary? (See Luke 1:26-38.)

• What was Mary's response?

As impossible as God's goal for Mary may have sounded to her (she would give birth to a son while still a virgin and her son would be the Savior of the world!), she responded, "Be it done to me according to your word" (Luke 1:38). That is to be our response to God's goals for us.

Knowing the Difference Between Goals and Desires. The secret to achieving God's goals is learning the difference between a godly goal and a godly desire. A *godly goal* is any specific choice reflecting God's purposes for your life that does not depend on people or circumstances beyond your ability or right to control—and you are the only person you have the ability or right to control. A *godly desire* is any specific choice that depends on the cooperation of other people or the success of events or favorable circumstances you cannot control.

• What are some of God's goals that cannot be blocked? (You can find three on page 83 of the text.)

• What can you gain by aligning your goals with God's goals and your desires with His desires?

Darcy would save herself a lot of grief if she changed her goal to make the cheerleading squad into a desire, and set herself the goal of doing her best in the tryouts and remaining a good friend to Brittany no matter what happens. No one can frustrate that goal except Darcy herself.

• What realigning can you do?

• What goals would you do well to change into desires?

• What godly goals can you replace those with?

When we work toward godly goals, we may have to deal with some disappointments, but we won't have to deal with the anger, anxiety or depression that comes when our happiness or success hinges on reaching a goal that can be blocked or that is uncertain or impossible.

GODLY GOALS CENTER ON BUILDING CHARACTER

God's basic goal for your life is character development: becoming the person He wants you to be. Because it's a godly goal, no one can block it but you—although every day you struggle against the world, the flesh and the devil and their opposition to your efforts to become a godly person.

• Read Romans 5:3-5 and James 1:24. What do Paul and James tell us about the opposition we face from the world, the flesh and the devil?

• When have you realized how God has used a trial or tribulation in your life to help shape you into the person He wants you to be?

• What do you think God is doing in your character through a current trial or tribulation?

Uncovering Wrong Goals. One of the great things about trials and tribulations is that they reveal wrong goals.

• When has a trial or tribulation revealed a wrong goal?

• Consider the trials and tribulations you are currently facing. What wrong goal might they be pointing to?

When we're going through a trial or tribulation, God doesn't offer us the kind of quick-fix solutions the world holds out. Instead, He uses those dark, difficult times of testing to bring us to the point of recognizing that we can totally rely on Him and Him alone to meet our needs. And that's a lesson definitely worth learning.

START STOMPING!

World, You've Got to Be Kidding! Choose one of the eight goals you looked at earlier: success, significance, fulfillment, satisfaction, happiness, fun, security and peace. Then illustrate—with your own drawing, with pictures from magazines, with details from life on campus—what the world says is the way to achieve that goal. How effective are the world's ideas? How long lasting is the success, significance, fulfillment, satisfaction, happiness, fun, security or peace that the world offers? Then consider God's means to that end. What do you think He wants you to do to achieve that goal? (Don't worry if you're not sure. Just stay tuned for the next chapter.)

The Fires of Life. Grab some orange construction paper and cut out tongues of flame. Use a piece of brown paper to make the logs that feed the fire. Now, on pieces of white paper, briefly describe those times in your life—those trials and temptations—when you've felt as if you've been in the fire. Where you can, note how God used that situation to teach you to rely more on Him and/or to shape you more into the person He wants you to be. Let those incidents where you can see what God was doing encourage you that He is just as involved in those other as-yet-inexplicable situations.

Story Time. It's not always easy to appreciate what God is doing in us when times are tough. Sometimes it's easier to appreciate the good that God is doing or has done through the hard times that other people have experienced. So get together with someone (a long-time believer like Mom or Dad or a pastor, prayer partner or leader in the church) who will tell you about a fiery time in life and what God did through that trial. Reviewing that time will probably be as encouraging for the person sharing the story as it is for you!

> *All this talk about godly goals and godly desires can be pretty confusing. I'm glad You make it clear that the basic goal You have for my life is for me to become the person You want me to be. God, help me to cooperate with that goal. Give me patience and hope when life is hard and doesn't make sense. I need to know that You're using those kinds of times for my good. I know that You're using those times to teach me to depend on You. I want to learn that—but please be merciful as You teach me. I pray in Jesus' name. Amen.*

STRENGTH GIVERS

These words are *for* you and *about* you! As you read each day's verse, ask yourself, "How would my life be different if I could live out this truth?"—and ask God to help you do so.

Monday:	Galatians 4:6-7
Tuesday:	Romans 8:14-15
Wednesday:	Romans 8:17
Thursday:	Romans 8:28
Friday:	Hebrews 4:16

God's Guidelines for the Walk of Faith

Along your own walk of faith, you'll see—as I (Dave) have—that God uses bad things to produce good results. Yes, it's hard for me to see Davers hurt, but I truly rejoice when I see the Christlike heart of compassion in my little boy.

- When have you seen God use something bad—in your life or in someone else's—to produce good results?

God cries with us when the bad things happen, but He also works to redeem them and make good come from them (see Romans 8:28). If we don't believe in this truth and in God's fundamental goodness, we can become bitter and unhappy. And the devil is more than willing to confuse our beliefs so that we'll grow distant from God. Let's take a look at the beliefs that keep us close to Him.

Proper Beliefs Lead to a Proper Walk

If Satan can muddy our minds and weaken our faith with partial truths, he can stop our effectiveness for God and stunt our growth as Christians. So let's look closely at what the Bible teaches about success, significance, fulfillment, satisfaction, happiness, fun, security and peace. Our beliefs about these things need to be anchored in the Scriptures if we are to walk with Jesus.

Success Comes from Right Goals. If you ranked yourself low in the success category of the Belief Quiz, you are probably having difficulty reaching your goals in life. And if you aren't reaching your goals, it's probably because you're working on the wrong goals.

- According to 2 Peter 1:5-7, what are seven goals for those of us who call ourselves "Christians"?

- What are the odds for reaching these goals—for achieving moral excellence, knowledge, self-control, perseverance, godliness, brotherly kindness and Christian love? Explain why you answered the way you did.

Focusing on God's goals will lead to success in God's terms. As these qualities increase in our lives, we will be useful and fruitful—and that's success!

- Notice what is not mentioned in Peter's discussion of success. No word is said about talents, intelligence or gifts that are not equally distributed to all believers. Why is this significant? Why is this encouraging?

Your self-worth is not determined by your talents, your intelligence or your gifts. Your self-worth is based on your identity in Christ and your growth in character, both of which are equally available to every Christian.

- What did you learn from Joshua about success in God's terms?

For Joshua, success hinged entirely on obedience to God—and that should be our pattern, too. When we accept God's goal for our lives and pursue it obediently, we'll become the people God wants us to be—and that's big-time success!

Significance Comes from Proper Use of Time. Significance is a time issue. What is forgotten as time passes is of little importance. What is remembered for eternity is of great importance (see 1 Corinthians 3:14; 1 Timothy 4:7-8).

- Consider a typical week. What activities are you involved in that will remain for eternity?

- What percentage of your time and energy go to those activities of eternal significance that you just listed?

- Read the story Jesus tells in Matthew 25:31-40. What does this parable teach about which activities are significant?

What we do and say for Christ, no matter how unimportant it seems in this world, will last forever. We have His word on that!

Fulfillment Comes from Serving Others. For the Christian, true fulfillment in life comes when we discover our unique gifts and abilities and use them to serve others and glorify the Lord (see 1 Peter 4:10).

- How can you serve God in your family—in your role as son or daughter, brother or sister? Be specific! And let the lesson of Matthew 25:31-40 cue you!

- How can you serve God at school and with your friends? These are your mission fields, and you are the person God has appointed to serve there.

Sadly, many people miss their calling in life by looking for fulfillment in the world. Find your fulfillment in the kingdom of God by deciding to be an ambassador for Christ in the world (see 2 Corinthians 5:20).

Satisfaction Comes from Living a Quality Life. Satisfaction results from living righteously and seeking to make everything we're involved in better. Satisfaction comes from doing our best for God, whatever it is we're doing.

- If you're not super satisfied with your life right now, take the quality/quantity test. Are you trying to do a few things well, or are you doing a lot of (too many?) things and just trying to hang on?

- Apply the quality/quantity yardstick to relationships, too. Are you investing in a few good friendships, or are you spreading yourself too thin and finding yourself with lots of acquaintances but no solid friend?

- What do your answers to the two preceding questions tell you about yourself?

- What changes in your life do they get you thinking about making?

The key to personal satisfaction is not gaining more responsibilities, but working hard and doing your best in the responsibilities you have. Likewise, personal satisfaction with relationships comes with following Jesus' example and investing in some close and quality relationships with people who will be there when you need them.

Happiness Comes from Wanting What You Have. The world says that happiness is having what we want, but God says, "Happy is the person who wants what he has."

- Which definition of happiness—the world's or God's— has the greatest influence over you right now?

- What's resulting from that influence?

- Satan's lie is that God won't give you what you need or enough of what you need. What area of your life is Satan lying to you about? Arm yourself against this attack by reading God's truth in Matthew 6:25-34.

Talk to God about what is blocking your happiness right now. Ask Him to change your focus, your heart and your values so that you can be happy in what He has given you. You have everything you need to make you happy forever: You have Christ, eternal life and the love of a heavenly Father who has promised to supply all your needs. If you really want to be happy, learn to be thankful for these gifts and everything else God has given you, not greedy for what you don't have.

Fun Comes from Enjoying Life Moment by Moment. Real fun is hanging loose and enjoying life as it happens, and the secret to enjoying life moment by moment is removing the roadblocks.

- Probably the biggest roadblock to Christian fun is our tendency to keep up appearances. Satan wants us to fear what people say and think about us. When has this roadblock been real for you?

- When have you, like King David, wanted to let loose and have fun but, unlike David, listened to the party poopers in your life and held back?

· Think about the last time you had fun. Was it a big, carefully planned event or a spur-of-the-moment activity? Why was it fun?

· Were you afraid of what people would think about you if you let yourself have fun? Why or why not?

· What else, if anything, keeps you from having fun? Let God know about these roadblocks to enjoying the gift of life and ask Him to show you how to avoid them and start having more fun.

Fear of what people think moves us to become people-pleasers. Be concerned about pleasing God—and let yourself enjoy the gift of life He's given you!

Security Comes from Focusing on Eternal Values. The key to experiencing security in our lives is to depend on things that will last for eternity, not just for a time.

· What are you depending on? Make a list below and then cross out those things that won't last forever.

_____

_____

_____

_____

_____

· What does your list—the way it looks now—tell you about yourself? Where will you start looking—and finding—real security?

· Security comes only from relating to that which is anchored in eternity, and one of those things is God's love. What does Paul teach about God's love in Romans 8:35-39?

Nothing—absolutely nothing—can separate us from the love of God! Now that's security! So the greatest security you can find comes with taking a firm grip on values and relationships that will endure as long as God Himself.

Peace Comes from Quieting the Inner Storm. The key to experiencing peace is the understanding that it is primarily an internal issue. We already have peace with God (see Romans 5:1), but the peace of God is something we need to turn to every day (see John 14:27).

- What does Philippians 4:6-7 teach about the peace God gives?

- When have you experienced a peace that passes understanding while the storms of life raged around you?

- What storms of life are raging around you now?

- What can you do—what will you do—to plug into the peace God offers you?

Nothing will happen to you today that God and you can't handle. Your daily time of worship, prayer and reading God's Word will help you find that peace of God you need and want.

START STOMPING!

"Before" and "After." Have you ever seen those ads for muscle-building drinks or anti-baldness remedies or fat-reducing concoctions? They often have a "before" and an "after" picture to try to convince you of the product's effectiveness. Well, come up with your own "before" and "after" poster illustrating the world's ideas of success, significance, fulfillment, satisfaction, happiness, fun, security and peace versus God's. Focusing on God's message like this will help you ignore the loud but wrong message of the world.

Take a Look in the Mirror. No, we don't mean a glass mirror. We mean the mirror of a friend who knows you well. Get together for a Coke and talk about who you guys are and what gifts God has given each of you. Ask your friend what strengths or talents he or she sees in you—and do the same for your friend. Then brainstorm ways you can use those gifts for God. If you love basketball, can you coach elementary kids at the YMCA after school? If you love kids, can you help out in the three-year-olds' Sunday School class? If you like to write or draw or do office work, can your church use you? Learn about yourself from a friend who knows you well and let him or her help you discover a new mission field!

It Sounds Corny, But... Count your blessings! Focusing on what we don't have means unhappiness. So focus right now for a few minutes on what you do have! On a piece of paper, race the clock and see how many blessings you can write down in 60 seconds—and I bet that won't be enough time! Look back on this list when the Madison Avenue ad makers, the cliques at school, or Satan himself are making you want more than what you have. On your mark! Get set! Go!

> *It makes a lot of sense, God. If I focus on Your goals for my life, I'll surely find success—the kind of success You want me to have. Yep, it makes a lot of sense and it sounds simple enough, but I'm not sure how easy it is to live out. Help me, God, to want for myself what You want for me—moral excellence, knowledge, self-control, perseverance, godliness, brotherly kindness and Christian love. And help me to be obedient to You as I work toward these goals. Thanks for these guidelines You give me for walking a life of faith in You and for giving me the power, through Your Spirit, to keep on walking. I pray in Jesus' name. Amen.*

STRENGTH GIVERS

These words are *for* you and *about* you! As you read each day's verse, ask yourself, "How would my life be different if I could live out this truth?"—and ask God to help you do so.

Monday:	1 Thessalonians 1:4
Tuesday:	2 Corinthians 5:14-15
Wednesday:	Jeremiah 29:11
Thursday:	Romans 8:38-39
Friday:	Colossians 2:7

WINNING THE BATTLE FOR YOUR MIND

Perhaps you're like Shelley—spiritually out of touch and defeated in your daily life. You may not realize that Satan is battling to control your mind and ruin your life. May this chapter help you realize that God can renew your mind and free you from the struggle.

GOD'S WAY VERSUS MAN'S WAY

Faith is God's way to live. Trying to think and reason without God is man's way to live. God's way (the high road) and man's way (the low road) are often in conflict.

The Two Paths. Let's consider some of the differences between these two paths.

- What does Proverbs 3:5-6 and Isaiah 55:9 teach you about the high road versus the low road?

- Why is the Bible important for walking the high road?

The Low Road. We walk the low road when we think thoughts and consider plans that conflict with what God's Word says, and doing so can slow our spiritual growth and block our maturity in Christ.

- Remember the example in the text? God's high road is honesty; the low road is cheating. When have you considered and even chosen the low road?

- What were the consequences of that decision? What did you learn from that incident?

- In what area(s) of your life do you tend to consider and even occasionally choose the low road?

• What will you do to get your thoughts back on the high road? (Don't worry if you're not sure at this point. That's what this chapter is all about!)

The Source of the Low Road. The two mains sources of low-road thoughts and ideas are our flesh (the part of us that was trained to live independently from God before we became Christians) and Satan.

• Think again about those areas of life where you feel especially susceptible to low-road thoughts and actions. What is behind that—your flesh, Satan or both?

• When have you been able to stand strong in the battle and choose the high road? What were the consequences of that decision? What did you learn from that incident?

You may feel helpless in this battle between the high road and the low road, but in each skirmish you are actually the one who determines which road to walk. Let's work now on a strategy you can use.

STRONGHOLDS ARE THE PRIME TARGET OF OUR WARFARE

In 2 Corinthians 10:3-5, Paul explains the battle for the mind.

• First, Paul states that the battle is not fought by human ability but by "divine power." Why does this make sense?

• Second, the main targets that must be destroyed are the "strongholds" in the mind, those bad patterns of thought that are burned into our minds either through repetition over time or through one-time, deeply shocking experiences. What strongholds are you aware of? (We'll look at several in a moment.)

Our Environment. You and I were born physically alive and spiritually dead in a world opposed to God's design. Before we came to Christ, all our experiences came from this sinful environment, and this environment influenced and shaped us.

- What people, places, movies, music or events have tempted you to travel the low road?

- What painful or even traumatic events (such as accidents or death) have drawn you to the low road?

We learned ways (which may or may not have been God's way) to cope with what happened to us and to solve the problems that resulted. When you became a Christian, your sins were washed away, but your old ways of thinking and behaving remained—a stronghold from your environment.

Temptation. When you feel attracted to the low-road plan instead of God's high-road plan for your life, you are experiencing temptation.

- Read Matthew 4:1-11. What temptations does Satan set before Jesus?

- What does Jesus do to stand strong against those low-road temptations?

- What can you learn from His example?

Satan knows just what buttons to push to tempt you away from depending on Christ. He knows where you are weak, and that's where he attacks.

Consideration and Choice. At the point when we're tempted to take the low road, we are on the threshold of a decision. If we don't immediately choose to "take captive every thought to make it obedient to Christ" (2 Corinthians 10:5, NIV), the likelihood of yielding to that temptation increases.

- Remember the "Cathy" cartoon? What happened when Cathy didn't immediately dismiss the tempting thought?

- When have you found yourself, like Cathy, hesitating at the threshold of decision and yielding to the low-road temptation? Give an example and say how you wish you would have handled it.

The Bible teaches that God has provided a way of escape from every temptation (see 1 Corinthians 10:13). But the escape is at the threshold—when the thought first occurs.

Action, Habit and Stronghold. People who study human behavior tell us that if we repeat an act for six weeks, it will become a habit. If we exercise that bad habit long enough, a stronghold (a low-road pattern of thinking) will be established.

- What strongholds have formed a groove in your mind? Circle any of these possibilities that apply and add your own.

      Hostility   Inferiority
      Inferiority   Manipulation
      Sexual addiction   Homosexuality
      Eating disorders   Others:

IN ORDER TO WIN THE BATTLE FOR YOUR MIND, YOU NEED A PLAN

Negative patterns of thinking and behavior that you've learned along the way don't need to control you.

Reprogramming. You can unlearn anything you've learned, and you can reprogram a mind that has been programmed wrong.

- What is the source of the wrong programming in your mind?

- Past experiences may have been spiritually or emotionally devastating. What can you do to start getting to know God as your loving Father and yourself as His accepted child?

Satan's Tricks. There's more going on in our minds than the bad patterns we've developed. We're also up against the devil.

- If Satan can place a thought in your mind—and he can— it isn't much more of a trick for him to make you think it's your idea. Why does Satan disguise his suggestions as our ideas?

- David, Ananias and Sapphira fell victim to ideas that Satan planted in their minds. Looking back on times you've stumbled, what idea was probably placed in your mind by Satan?

If Satan can get you to believe a lie, he can control your life—but you can have victory over Satan. By hearing God's Word being taught, studying your Bible and living as Christ's disciple, you can experience God's transforming and healing touch on your life. Let's develop a more specific plan.

EXPOSE THE LIE AND YOU WIN THE BATTLE

Satan's power is the lie. He has no power over us except what we give him when we don't take every thought captive and hold it up next to God's truth before believing and acting on it.

Truth. Since Satan's primary weapon is the lie, our defense against him is the truth. Before we outline a specific plan of defense, write out the truths of these three passages and personalize them. (For instance, in John 8:32, what bondage will God's truth free you from?)

John 8:32

_____
_____
_____
_____

John 17:15,17

_____
_____
_____
_____

Ephesians 6:14

_____

_____

_____

_____

Now let's look at your part in the battle.

Renew. First, you must be transformed by the renewing of your mind (see Romans 12:2). According to the following verses, how do you renew your mind?

Colossians 3:15

_____

_____

_____

_____

Colossians 3:16

_____

_____

_____

_____

- What are you doing to give your mind a steady diet of God's Word?

As you continue to fill your mind with God's truth, you will become better equipped to recognize the lie and take it captive.

Prepare for Action. Second, prepare your mind for action (see 1 Peter 1:13).

- What's the risk of dreaming and fantasizing?

- What good can come from dreaming and imagining—and what does that good result hinge on?

If you imagine yourself traveling the high road by obeying God's truth, you can move yourself toward living that way. Just be sure to follow through by doing what you imagine.

Captivate. Third, take every thought captive and make it obedient to Christ (see 2 Corinthians 10:5).

• What does this instruction mean in real life? Be specific.

• When have you successfully recognized a thought as counter to God's Word and been able to refuse it lodging in your brain? Let the example (or two or three) you come up with give you strength the next time a thought arises that needs to be rejected.

When a thought pops into your mind that doesn't agree with God's Word, refuse it immediately. Say aloud, "In Jesus' name, leave! I'm a child of God." Choose instead to believe and act on the truth.

Turn to God. Fourth, turn to God.

• What does Philippians 4:6 say?

• Why is praying aloud the smart thing to do when your commitment to the high road is being challenged by low-road thoughts from the world, the flesh or the devil?

When we pray, we acknowledge God and expose our thoughts to His truth. Furthermore, as we turn to God, He will do His part. Victory in the battle for our minds is the inheritance of everyone who is in Christ.

START STOMPING!

Construction Zone! What can you make to remind you to choose the high road of life? If you're good with words, come up with a slogan or write a poem. If you like art, make a poster. If you want something even more hands-on, do a 3-D road. Maybe making a bracelet or a bookmark is more your kind of thing. Whatever you do, put your "high road" wherever it can encourage you to choose that route throughout your day.

Give It Six Weeks, and Then . . . We've talked about bad thought patterns, knee-jerk reactions and habits that have taken root in your life, and you've learned what to do about those. Now think for a moment about a good habit you would like to develop over the next six weeks (a regular Bible study time, an exercise schedule, a Scripture memorization program, whatever!)—and do a six-week experiment. It just may stick! You've got nothing to lose by trying!

Make It Real. Read Philippians 4:8-9 again and then make it real. If you're a words person, list some specifics to flesh out those categories Paul calls you to think about. If you're more into scissors and glue, make a collage to illustrate things that are honorable, right, pure, lovely, of good repute, excellent and worthy of praise. You'll have an easier time tuning out the world's loud and strong voice if you can quickly replace it with the kinds of thoughts God wants His people to have.

> *It makes me angry, God, to think that Satan can put ideas in my head and then make me think they're my own. No wonder they call him the deceiver! He's playing hard ball! But I'm glad that, in You, I can have victory in this battle. I'm glad that You give me Your Word so that I can know the truth. I ask You to loosen those strongholds that keep me in bondage. And help me be a more able warrior when it comes to taking my thoughts captive and making them obedient to Christ. It's in His name I pray. Amen.*

STRENGTH GIVERS

These words are *for* you and *about* you! As you read each day's verse, ask yourself, "How would my life be different if I could live out this truth?"—and ask God to help you do so.

Monday:	Colossians 2:11
Tuesday:	1 Peter 5:8
Wednesday:	Colossians 1:13
Thursday:	Ephesians 3:12
Friday:	Philippians 4:8-9

You Must Be Real in Order to Be Right

Is there a little bit of Matthew in you?

- Is your sense of self-worth dependent on your performance in a certain area?

- What do you tend to do with your negative feelings about yourself or about life in general?

- What did you learn from Matthew's experience? What encouragement do you find in his story?

Matthew had some wrong beliefs, and when Satan convinced him to stuff his feelings inside, he couldn't discover that those beliefs were based on lies. As soon as Matthew recognized his false beliefs and got rid of them, his depression lifted.

Our Emotions Reveal What We're Thinking

In general, our emotions are a product of our thought life. If we don't think right—if we don't see God accurately and clearly understand His Word—we won't feel right.

Jeremiah's Story. Is there a little bit of Jeremiah in you?

- Do you feel as if God is against you?

- What problems are you seeing Him as the cause of?

- Are you feeling trapped by certain circumstances that are occuring in your life?

• Are you feeling afraid to trust God to protect you and therefore afraid of what life holds?

At this point, Jeremiah's beliefs about God are off because of the pain he's suffering. God wasn't the cause of his problems—and He isn't the cause of yours. But Jeremiah wasn't thinking right, believing right or seeing his circumstances right, so he wasn't feeling right either.

• Look again at Lamentations 3:19-24. What emotions does Jeremiah express here?

• What caused the turnaround?

• What lesson can you learn from Jeremiah?

Once Jeremiah was honest with God about his pain and his feelings, his wrong thinking became right thinking and his emotions followed.

What You See Is What You Think. We are not shaped as much by what's happening around us as we are by how we view what's happening around us. Life's events don't control who we are. God determines who we are, and our view of life's events determines how well we handle the pressures of life.

• Think about the last event that got you really down on yourself. What was your perspective on that event? Why did your view of that event lead you to feel so bad?

• Looking back at that same event, what perspective would have helped you deal with the situation and prevented such negative feelings about yourself?

Although we have very little control over our feelings, we do have control over our thoughts, and our thoughts determine our feelings and how we act. That's why it is so important to fill our minds with knowledge of God and His Word.

• Our feelings always react to what we think is true, whether it's true or not! Thinking your parents won't let you buy a car brings out different emotions than realizing the truth that they are going to buy the car for you, doesn't it? What half-truth or full-on lie do you believe about certain circumstances in your life? (Don't hesitate to call on a trusted friend or pastor to help you answer this question.)

Now determine (again, help is allowed and even encouraged!) God's truth about the situation. Think hard about that truth and let that right thinking guide your feelings. The order of Scripture is to know the truth, believe it, walk according to it and let our emotions be a result of our obedience. When you believe what you feel instead of the truth, you can't help but stumble in your walk of faith.

DON'T IGNORE THE WARNING SIGNS OF YOUR EMOTIONS

Our emotions are to our souls what our physical feelings are to our bodies. Just as physical pain keeps us from more serious injury and infection, emotions such as anger, sorrow and joy let us know what's going on inside.

- What do you usually do with your feelings?

- What attitude toward feelings did you grow up with?

- Are feelings good? Bad? Just part of being human? What happened to help shape your attitude toward feelings?

Now hear the truth. Feelings are neither good nor bad. They're just part of being human. Just as you respond to the warnings of physical pain, you need to learn to respond to emotional warning signals. Each of us can choose from among the following three options: (1) stuffing our emotions, (2) letting it all hang out, or (3) acknowledging our emotions.

Stuffing Our Emotions. We stuff our emotions when we ignore our feelings. This is the choice not to deal with them.

- According to David's account in Psalm 32:3,6, what happens when we stuff our feelings?

• How has your body reacted when you've stuffed your feelings? Have you experienced headaches? Nausea? Sleeplessness? Loss of appetite?

• Why do you sometimes choose to stuff your feelings?

• What truth about who God is can encourage you to open up to Him about what you're feeling? (See, for instance, Psalm 51:1 and Romans 8:38-39.)

Problems can seem bigger than God, but they never are. Know that truth—and know, too, that bottling up your feelings can hurt you and short-circuit your relationship with God. Stuffing your emotions is not a wise or healthy choice.

Letting It All Hang Out. Another unhealthy way to deal with emotions is to let them all hang out, telling anybody and everybody exactly how you feel.

• When have you lost control of your emotions and exploded with hurtful words and anger?

• Was that outburst healthy for you? Why or why not?

• Was your outburst healthy for those around you? Explain.

• What guidelines for dealing with anger does God give in Ephesians 4:26 and James 1:19-20?

Take comfort that the apostle Peter also got into trouble due to unbridled expressions of his feelings. Nevertheless, God used him in the New Testament church, evidence of the kind of powerful change that the Holy Spirit can produce in us.

Acknowledging Our Emotions. If we go to prayer feeling angry, depressed or frustrated, but pretend to be happy, God isn't pleased. He already knows how we feel. If we're not real, we're not right.

• Read again David's prayer for (against!) his enemies in Psalm 109:8-13. What surprises you most about his words?

- What comfort do you find from David's honest expression of his feelings? What does his example give you permission to do?

- When we are open with God about our feelings, we aren't so much at risk of clobbering ourselves or other people with them. What emotions do you need to honestly acknowledge before God right now? Take 3 minutes (or 33 minutes) and do so. After all, He already knows exactly what you're feeling—and He loves you anyway!

Being honest with God is crucial to your mental and spiritual health. So is being honest with a trusted friend or two.

With whom can you be totally honest emotionally? Do you let yourself do so? If you're not sure there's anyone in your life right now with whom you can be emotionally honest, make that a topic of prayer. Ask God to help you take the risk of trusting your feelings to someone—and ask Him to bring that person into your life.

Paul and even Jesus Himself modeled having a few intimate friendships with people who can help you through the emotions and struggles of life's hard times. Don't hesitate to follow their examples. Be open and honest with God and with one or two trusted friends. It's crucial for your mental health.

EMOTIONAL HONESTY: HOW TO DISH IT OUT AND HOW TO TAKE IT

We can acknowledge that emotional honesty is important, but living out that truth is not always easy. It's not always easy to be honest, and it's not always easy to deal with another person's honesty.

Dealing with Emotional Honesty. One of our challenges in the area of emotions is learning to respond to others when they honestly tell us their feelings.

- Do you shy away from people in pain because you worry about not having the right words? What does my (Neil's) experience tell you?

- When has someone come alongside you in your pain and cried with you? What did that action mean to you?

• What specific acts of kindness have encouraged you when you've gone through hard times?

Words aren't the important issue when someone is experiencing great inner pain. We shouldn't respond to their words; we should respond to their pain (see Romans 12:15).

Dishing Emotional Honesty. While it's challenging to deal with other people's emotional honesty, we also face challenges when it comes to being emotionally honest ourselves. Here are some guidelines. First, when it comes to acknowledging emotions, honesty is the best policy—but speak the truth in love (see Ephesians 4:15). Second, know your limits and give yourself permission to delay making a decision or talking through an issue until you've calmed down emotionally. Finally, recognize that a lot of physical factors (hunger, tiredness, hormones) affect your emotional limits.

• Which truth have you learned the hard way in life?

• Which guideline do you most need to work on?

• What will you do the next time you have emotions you want to share honestly with someone?

• Who is someone trustworthy of your honesty? Thinking through the possible scenario ahead of time can help you act the way you want to—and the way God wants you to!

The important process of renewing your mind includes acknowledging your emotions honestly and expressing them in love. Dealing with your emotions properly is an important step in keeping the devil from gaining a place in your life.

START STOMPING!

What You Think Is What You Feel. Still trying to get a handle on the fact that emotions follow thoughts? It's true, and recognizing that fact may keep you from becoming your own worst enemy as you deal with the ups and downs of life. Practice seeing the thoughts-precede-emotions pattern with these three scenarios:

1. The cashier at McDonald's can't even crack a smile and seems to growl when asking whether you want fries with your burger. What thoughts lead you to feel down on yourself? To feel compassion for the cashier?

2. You'd studied hard for the biology test but the questions seemed to be from a different chapter, if not an entirely different book. What thoughts cause you to beat yourself up mercilessly? What thoughts help you accept the results and strive to do better next time?

3. The relationship had been going well—at least that was your perspective. What thoughts lead to depression? What thoughts lead to sadness rather than a total lack of self-worth?

It's Not Just for Trains. Get with a friend and blow off steam! That may mean playing a game of one-on-one basketball, or going for a hard run, or (fill in the blank). God won't mind what you do as long as you don't hurt yourself or anyone else. He already knows what's inside!

Random Acts of Kindness. Who in your life needs some kindness today? Someone who's having a bad day? Someone who's received the fallout from some of your "emotional honesty"? (First apologize and ask for forgiveness. Then be kind!) Someone who serves behind the scenes and could use a pat on the back? Someone in your family whom you'd rather tease than be nice to? Choose a person and a random act of kindness for each day of the week. (For ideas, consider who that person is, but also look above at your answer to the question, "What specific acts of kindness have encouraged you when you've gone through hard times?") But be warned. This kind of behavior can be gratifying to the point of addiction!

I guess it shouldn't surprise me that You who made me and who gave me my emotions don't mind hearing about them. I'm relieved, God, to learn I don't have to hide from You or pretend to be something I'm not. It seems awkward to be angry or depressed or frustrated or irritable with You, but I know You can help me deal with those things. Teach me to be honest with my emotions—and to be loving when I am. Help me learn to listen to my emotions and understand what

*they're telling me. And, God, give me a friend who will accept me
and all my crazy emotions—and help me be that kind of friend, too.
I pray in Jesus' name. Amen.*

STRENGTH GIVERS

These words are *for* you and *about* you! As you read each day's
verse, ask yourself, "How would my life be different if I could live
out this truth?"—and ask God to help you do so.

Monday:	Colossians 3:4
Tuesday:	Galatians 3:26,28
Wednesday:	Ephesians 4:15
Thursday:	Ephesians 4:26
Friday:	Romans 12:15

HEALING EMOTIONAL WOUNDS FROM YOUR PAST

Look again at the story of Cindy and Dan.

- What misunderstanding of Romans 8:28 did Cindy have?

- What did I (Neil) explain to Cindy—and you—about God's promise in that verse?

- What truth (it's a recurring theme in this book!) did Cindy need to get a grip on before she could be free of the crippling effect of being raped?

Jesus Christ, not our past hurts, determines our identity. When Cindy learned that, she was able to move on from the rape and serve the Lord. Are you still working on learning that lesson? The next few pages can help.

BAD THINGS DO HAPPEN TO GOOD PEOPLE

All of us have a number of hurtful, upsetting experiences in our past that have scarred us emotionally. And one or more of the events may have caused deep inner pain that has hindered your growth as a Christian.

- What bad things have happened to you?

- What feelings do you still have as a result of one or more of the events you listed?

We're calling these long-term feelings, which hide deep inside you, *primary emotions*, and their power is determined by our past experiences. The more painful the experience, the more powerful the primary emotion. Anything in the present that links you with your past experience can trigger those primary emotions.

- What can trigger the primary emotions you listed above—certain words, situations, smells, topics of conversation, dates, locations, activities, and so forth?

We can't completely isolate ourselves from triggers, so we need to learn how to resolve past hurts.

LEARNING TO RESOLVE PRIMARY EMOTIONS

We have no control over a primary emotion when it is triggered—so don't feel guilty when those emotions arise.

True Thinking. True thinking about the trigger can help you deal with the emotions you're feeling as a result of that trigger.

- When has someone (like the football player talking to his meathead teammate) helped straighten out your thinking when emotions were overwhelming you?

- What kind of right thinking can you arm yourself with in anticipation of experiencing once again the primary feelings you know are lurking inside?

Coping. Think for a moment about how you are coping with serious hurts in the past.

- Which options have you chosen or are you choosing?

  ___ You have no conscious memory of the pain.
  ___ You avoid people or experiences that bring back bad memories.
  ___ You remember what happened but you act as though it never did.
  ___ You try to cover up the pain with food, drugs or sex.
  ___ Other (list):

_____

_____

_____

- God is light. What does He want us to do with pain from the past?

God knows our hidden hurts, and He knows that His light—His love, His truth, His power—can bring healing to those hurts. If those dark areas are beyond conscious memory right now, trust that God will bring them to light at the right time.

SEE YOUR PAST IN THE LIGHT OF WHO YOU ARE

God gives us two guidelines when it comes to resolving the painful experiences of the past. First, look at those experiences in light of who you are now as opposed to who you were then.

- Why is this a good guideline for resolving pain from the past?

- What truth does God give you in 2 Corinthians 5:17 to help you follow this guideline?

- How have you resolved the question, "Where was God when all this was going on?"

"Where was God when all this was going on?" is a fair question to ask God—He knows you're thinking about it anyway. As you ask this question and wait for an answer, accept the truth that God was with you when others hurt you or when you made some bad choices. Beyond that, let the answer be a mystery this side of heaven.

- What can God do for you in the present despite the deep hurts?

God is in your life right now desiring to set you free from your past. You can't fix your past, but you can let God set you free from it. Seeing past events through your identity in Christ is what starts the healing, freeing process.

FORGIVE THOSE WHO HAVE HURT YOU IN THE PAST

The second step toward resolving the painful experiences of the past is to forgive those who have hurt you.

Why Should I Forgive Them? But why should you forgive the one(s) who hurt you? Let's look at three reasons.

- First, forgiveness is required by God. What does Jesus teach in Matthew 6:14-15?

- Second, forgiveness is necessary to avoid being trapped by Satan (see 2 Corinthians 2:10-11 and Ephesians 4:26-27). How can Satan use our lack of forgiveness to trap us and cause greater pain and suffering?

- Third, forgiveness is to be the normal way of life for all Christians. Why do we as Christians need to be forgiving people?

Forgiveness frees us from the past. Forgiveness keeps our relationship with God open. And forgiveness needs to characterize all our relationships because all of us need forgiveness.

What Is Forgiveness? In order to understand what forgiveness is, we must first see what it is not.

- List two or three things that forgiveness is not and circle those that are new to you.

_____

_____

_____

_____

_____

Forgiveness is not forgetting. Forgiveness is not putting up with someone's sin; it isn't being a doormat or continually allowing yourself to be hurt by another. And forgiveness is not revenge or a demand for repayment.

- Forgiveness means deciding to live with the consequences of another person's sin (something you're doing whether or not you forgive the one who hurt you). What is freeing about this definition? What freedom will you find if you decide to live with the consequences of another person's sin?

You can choose to live in bitterness and unforgiveness or, by deciding not to hold the offense against the offender, in peace and forgiveness. The latter, of course, is God's way.

Twelve Steps to Forgiveness. We don't truly forgive someone without admitting the hurt and hatred involved. But until you forgive, you will continue to be hurt because you have not released yourself from the past. Forgiveness is the only way to stop the pain, and here are 12 steps you can walk through to forgiveness. Let's look at them closely.

1. Write on a sheet of paper the names of the persons who hurt you.

   - Why do you think it is important to be specific?

   - Why is it wise to get God involved in this step?

   - Why do you and God probably need to be on this list of people you need to forgive?

2. Face the hurt and the hate.

   - It's not a sin to admit the reality of your emotions. In fact, why is it healthy to write down how you feel about these people and their offenses?

3. Realize that the cross of Christ makes forgiveness possible, fair and right.

   - Why is this important fact crucial for your journey to forgiveness?

4. Decide that you will bear the burden of each person's sin (see Galatians 6:1-2).

- Write what this step means in your own words—and explain why it is key to true forgiveness.

5. Decide to forgive.

- What does this step suggest about the relationship between feelings, the will, and actions when it comes to forgiveness?

6. Take your list to God and pray the following: "I forgive [name] for [list of offense(s)]."

- Why is it important not to rush through this step?

7. Destroy the list.

- What does this step represent?

8. Do not expect that your decision to forgive will result in major changes in the other persons.

- Whom will your decision to forgive have the greatest impact on? Why?

- What are we called to do regarding those people we are forgiving?

9. Try to understand the people you have forgiven.

- What do you know about the people who have hurt you that helps you understand that they have been hurt, too?

- Why is this an important step to take toward freeing yourself from bitterness?

10. Expect positive results of forgiveness in you.

- What are some of the positive results that can come with extending forgiveness to those who have hurt you?

11. Thank God for the lessons you have learned and the maturity you have gained as a result of your decision to forgive the offenders (see Romans 8:28-29).

    • What lessons can be learned from forgiving those who have offended you? And why is forgiveness a step toward maturity?

12. Be sure to accept your part of the blame.

    • What action often needs to follow accepting responsibility (see Matthew 5:23-26)?

Forgive and Be Free. Forgiveness really can heal the hurts of the past.

    • Read again the account of Corrie ten Boom facing a guard from her Nazi concentration camp. What message did God have for you personally in this story?

When we forgive, we throw off the chains of bitterness and start the process of healing emotions that have been damaged. When we have forgiven the people who have hurt us, we find that we have really set ourselves free.

START STOMPING!

Live and Learn. Bad things do happen to good people. Bad things do happen to God's people. Talk to someone who has walked with God a long time, through good times and bad. Ask that person to share what God taught him or her through those bad times. Ask that brother or sister in the Lord what he or she has learned along the way about forgiveness and the freedom that comes with forgiving.

A Picture Is Worth . . . You've read a lot of words about bondage to pain from the past and the freedom that comes from forgiveness. Make that contrast more real for yourself by drawing a picture, writing a poem, creating a collage, fashioning a sculpture, putting a new tune together—anything that will help remind you in a tangible way the transformation from bondage and darkness to freedom and light that is available when we obey the command to forgive. (Like all of God's commands, this one is given for your benefit!)

Take a Walk. Review the 12 steps to forgiveness and start walking. This path will indeed take you to the point where the pain from the past no longer has a hold on you. You will probably always remember the incident, but the intense emotion will be gone. It's a gift of grace from God who heals. These 12 steps show you how to receive that gift.

> *God, this forgiveness stuff is a tall order! I'm glad You're by my side to help me walk the path I need to walk to be free from the pain of the past. Please be at work in my spirit to make me want to forgive. Give me the strength I need to choose to forgive. And, as You did for Corrie ten Boom, transform my heart so that I can reach out—at least in prayer—to those who have hurt me. And as I walk this path to forgiveness, make me very aware of all that You've forgiven me for and all that You continue to forgive me for, and may that awareness motivate me to give to others the kind of forgiveness You have given to me. I pray in Jesus' name. Amen.*

STRENGTH GIVERS

These words are *for* you and *about* you! As you read each day's verse, ask yourself, "How would my life be different if I could live out this truth?—and ask God to help you do so.

Monday:	Matthew 6:14-15
Tuesday:	Romans 8:1
Wednesday:	Galatians 5:1,13-15
Thursday:	1 Corinthians 2:12
Friday:	Colossians 3:1-4

DEALING WITH REJECTION IN YOUR RELATIONSHIPS

Everyone knows what it feels like to be criticized and rejected at times, even by the very people in our lives we desperately want to please.

- What experiences and people come to mind when you hear the word "rejection"?

- How do you usually deal with rejection?

- How would you like to be able to deal with rejection?

God Himself rejected us until we were accepted by Him in Christ at salvation (see Romans 15:7). Since then we have been the target of Satan, the accuser, who never stops lying to us about how worthless we are to God and others.

- What role do you think Satan plays to the feelings of rejection you live with? Why would he want you to focus on feelings and experiences of rejection?

In this life we all have to live with the pain and pressure of rejection—but we don't have to let that pain and pressure cripple us or our growth in Christ.

WHEN YOU ARE CRITICIZED OR REJECTED

We have several options when it comes to dealing with rejection, but unfortunately we all learned early in life to take one of three defensive (and ineffective) positions.

Beat the System. Some people defend themselves against rejection by buying into the dog-eat-dog system and learning to compete and scheme to get ahead.

- Are you dealing with rejection by trying to earn acceptance through your performance? Are you driven to do everything right? Are you unable to let anyone get close to you? Are you worried and stressed out most of the time?

- Even if this isn't your defensive position of choice, evaluate the effectiveness of this option. Why does or doesn't it work?

- How can this "beat the system" approach impact a person's relationship with God?

Beat-the-system controllers are some of the most insecure people you'll ever meet. And, sadly, their defensive strategy only leads to more rejection. Others soon begin to resent these people for their self-centered living.

Give in to the System. Many people respond to rejection by simply giving in to it. They continue to try to satisfy others, but their failures drive them to believe that they really are unlovable and that being rejected makes sense.

- Where, if at all, are you buying into someone's false judgment of your worth? Which of the world's false values lead you to self-condemnation and feelings of inferiority?

- Even if this isn't your defensive position of choice, evaluate the effectiveness of this option. Why does or doesn't it work?

- How can this "give in to the system" approach impact a person's relationship with God?

By giving in to the world's false judgment, people who accept the world's standards of worth and realize they don't measure up can only look forward to more and more rejection. In fact, having bought the world's lie, they even reject themselves, leading them to question or doubt any acceptance that might come their way.

Rebel Against the System. Rebels and dropouts respond to rejection by saying, "I don't need you or your love." Although deep inside they crave acceptance, these people refuse to admit their needs.

- Are you a rebel or a dropout when it comes to dealing with rejection? Do you feel a lot of self-hatred and bitterness and often wish you'd never been born?

- Are you irresponsible and undisciplined, rebelling against everyone and everything despite the fact that you're hurting yourself by doing so?

- Even if this isn't your defensive position of choice, evaluate the effectiveness of this option. Why does or doesn't it work?

- How can this "rebel" approach impact a person's relationship with God?

The attitude and behavior of people who rebel tend to alienate others and push them to defend the system being rejected. The rebels' responses to those who reject them breed further rejection.

Defensiveness Is Defenseless. As long as we live on this earth we will experience rejection. How should we respond to it? Should we try to defend ourselves? No—for two reasons.

- First, if you are in the wrong, you don't have a defense. What happens—as hard as it may be to do—when you simply respond to an accusation with, "You're right; I was wrong"?

- Second, if you are right, you don't need a defense. What does Jesus model for you in this regard? (See 1 Peter 2:23.)

If you find yourself responding to rejection defensively, try focusing your attention on those things that will build up and establish your faith.

- What are some specific things—things that can build up your faith—you can think about the next time you feel rejected or unworthy?

The world's system for determining your value as a person is not what determines your value. Your allegiance is to Christ your Lord, not to the world, and He is the reason you are worthy.

WHEN YOU ARE TEMPTED TO CRITICIZE OR REJECT OTHERS

Rejection is a two-way street: You can receive it and you can give it. We've looked at the first. Now let's look at how to respond to the temptation to tear up others with criticism or rejection.

- What message does God have for you in Romans 14:4 and Philippians 2:3?

- Think about your relationships for a moment. Are you in line with what God's Word says in Romans 14:4 and Philippians 2:3, or do you tend to attack people's character rather than taking responsibility for your own?

- Do you tend to be absorbed with your own needs instead of looking out for your friends' needs?

- What do you need to confess and repent?

Instead of devoting ourselves to developing our own characters and meeting each other's needs, we often yield to Satan's prodding to criticize each other and selfishly meet our own needs. We need to practice what God's Word says if we are to grow up in Christ and glorify Him in our friendships.

Focus on Responsibilities. Satan has deceived us in our relationships by tempting us to focus on our rights instead of on our responsibilities.

- Think about your relationship with your parents. What happens when you focus on your rights?

- What happens when you focus on your responsibility to be an obedient son or daughter? (If you can't answer this second question, find out!)

- Now think about your relationship with a friend. What happens when you focus on your rights?

- What happens when you focus on your responsibility to be the kind of friend to your friend that you want him or her to be to you? (Yes, that's a loose paraphrase of the Golden Rule.)

Keep in mind that God is more concerned about how well we fulfill our responsibilities, not whether we receive everything we feel we have coming to us.

Don't Play the Role of Conscience. Sometimes we may be tempted to play the role of the conscience or even the Holy Spirit in someone else's life.

- Why is being another person's conscience sometimes tempting?

- How do you feel when someone plays conscience for you?

Our job as God's representatives on this planet is to surround people with acceptance and let the Holy Spirit do His job of convicting in His time.

Discipline Yes, Judgment No. We are required by God to confront and restore Christians who have clearly violated Scripture (see Matthew 18:15-16) but we are not allowed to judge their characters.

- How would you react to "You're a liar," a statement about your character? To "You just told a lie," a statement about your behavior? Why would you react differently?

- Do you tend to confront? Judge? Or avoid the issue entirely? What would God have you do—and how?

We must care enough about people to confront their sinful behaviors, but we should never tear down their characters.

Express Your Needs Without Judging. It's okay to express your needs to others, but it's important to do so without slamming them in the process.

- How do you respond to a "you" accusation ("You never call.")?

- How do you respond to an "I" message ("I miss it when you don't call regularly.")?

- Think about your own speech patterns. Which is more common—the "you" accusation or the "I" message? How do people respond to your pattern?

We all have basic human needs to feel loved, accepted and worth-while. The bases for Satan's work of temptation in your life are real needs that are not being met.

- What makes it tough for you to express your needs in a proper way?

- What need(s) would you share and allow other people to meet if you were willing to take the risk of stepping out from behind your mask?

- What's the worst thing that could happen if you took that step of risk? Could you survive?

- What's the best thing that could happen if you told someone what you really need right now? Is that possible result worth the risk?

By not letting other believers meet our legitimate needs, we are act-ing independently of God and leave ourselves vulnerable to the world, the flesh and the devil. We are also robbing people of the opportunity to minister to our needs.

- When have you had the opportunity to minister to some-one in need?

- What did you feel like when you were able to help? That's the gift you give when you are open and willing to let someone help you!

God works in our lives through committed Christian relationships. So the next time you're tempted to find character defects and performance flaws in another believer, ask for the grace of God to see beyond those externals. After all, isn't that what you want others to do for you?

START STOMPING!

Yikes! Who's That in the Mirror? What did you learn about yourself from your study of Romans 14:4 and Philippians 2:3? To whom do you need to apologize? Choose one person on your list and do it today! As part of your apology, you may want to let him or her know that you're learning about what God wants in our relationships with others.

The "I"s Have It. What will you say in the following situations? (Practicing "I" messages just may help one pop out the next time a "you" accusation would fly!)

- At the last minute, your friend once again cancels plans with you to be with his or her girlfriend or boyfriend instead.

- Your mother comments on what you're wearing as you're heading out the door and it feels like criticism.

- Your dad focuses on your C+ in math instead of the English grade you worked hard to pull up.

What Have You Got to Lose? It feels pretty good to have God love you through His people, so dive in! Be wise in whom you choose, but find someone to tell about a need you have right now. Get together with the person before seven days go by. And give yourself permission to start the conversation with, "This is really hard for me . . ." Don't be surprised when God richly blesses you with warm acceptance and love. That's just the kind of God He is!

> *God, You've clearly shown me what You want from my relationships with other people—and I've seen how easy it is for me to be critical instead of taking responsibility for myself. I've also seen how self-centered I can be. Please forgive me—and please change me! Give me, I ask, the grace to not be defensive when I'm rejected, the grace to express my needs without judging the people who are letting me down, and especially the grace to see people as You see them. I guess what I'm saying is "Help me live by Your Golden Rule." I ask that in Jesus' name. Amen.*

STRENGTH GIVERS

These words are *for* you and *about* you! As you read each day's verse, ask yourself, "How would my life be different if I could live out this truth?"—and ask God to help you do so.

Monday:	Matthew 7:12
Tuesday:	Galatians 6:2
Wednesday:	Ephesians 4:1
Thursday:	Hebrews 3:1
Friday:	1 John 3:11,16

PEOPLE GROW BETTER TOGETHER

Have you ever thought about Christianity as a team sport? Alone we can easily get discouraged on our Christian walk, but together we find strength as we encourage each other, pray for each other and build each other up.

- When has a team of believers helped you through an especially difficult time?

- How did the believers show they cared? What support did they offer you?

- Shifting from the receiving end, what did you do to contribute to the functioning of the team and the well-being of other team members?

- If you've never been part of a team of believers—a youth group, a church—what's keeping you back? Busyness? No driver's license? Wanting to be cool or not wanting to be a nerd? Be honest with yourself about your reasons—and listen carefully for what God wants for you.

A church youth group is a place where you can share your concerns, a place where people really care about you and a place where you and your Christian friends can help each other grow as disciples of Jesus Christ. A church youth group is the place for you if you're serious about your faith.

DISCIPLESHIP: THE HEARTBEAT OF GROWTH AND MATURITY

Discipleship is the intensely personal activity of two or more persons helping each other experience a growing relationship with God. And such caring and growing together is what being Christ's disciples is all about.

Disciple and *Discipler.* You are both a disciple and a discipler in your Christian relationships.

- In what relationships are you more the disciple than the discipler? What have those relationships helped you to learn?

- In what relationships are you more the discipler than the disciple? What have you learned in those particular relationships?

Counselor and *Counselee.* You also have the opportunity to be a peer counselor and to receive counsel in your Christian relationships.

- When has God guided you through the counsel of a fellow believer? Be specific.

- When has God used you to offer His truth to someone who was in need of counsel? What did you learn from that experience?

As a believer, you are disciple as well as discipler, counselor as well as counselee. The following designs for discipleship and concepts for counseling offer some practical guidelines for your ministry to others.

DESIGNS FOR DISCIPLESHIP

In Colossians 2:6-10, Paul outlines three levels in the ministry of discipling others. Each step of the way, sin, the world, the flesh and the devil can interfere. These points of conflict must be resolved and replaced by specific steps of growth.

Level 1: Identity. Here, people establish and come to understand their identity in Christ (see Colossians 2:10).

- What does the person being discipled need to learn in each of the following areas of life in order to establish his or her identity in Christ?

Spiritual life

_____
_____
_____
_____
_____

Mind

_____
_____
_____
_____
_____

Emotions

_____
_____
_____
_____
_____

Will

_____
_____
_____
_____
_____

Relationships

_____
_____
_____
_____
_____

- If you are working to establish your identity in Christ, which area(s) would you like help in? Whom can you go to for discipling? Ask your youth pastor for suggestions.

- If you feel solid about your identity in Christ, think back to who helped you to get to this point. Whom can you thank?

And whom can you help disciple? Let your youth pastor know of your willingness to be a discipler.

Level 2: Maturity. At this level, believers become mature in their faith and are "built up in [Christ]" (Colossians 2:7).

• What does the person being discipled need to learn in each of teh following areas of life in order to become more Christlike?

Spiritual life

_____

_____

_____

_____

Mind

_____

_____

_____

_____

Emotions

_____

_____

_____

_____

Will

_____

_____

_____

_____

Relationships

_____

_____

_____

- If you're confident about who you are in Christ and now are working to become more mature in your faith, which area(s) would you like help in? Whom can you go to for discipling? Ask your youth pastor for suggestions.

- Even if you've been a believer for a while, you may still be working on some of these areas. Which ones would you like some discipling help in? For which areas could you be a discipler? Talk to your youth pastor about both your needs and your willingness to minister.

Many new Christians want to know right away, "What should I do to grow as a Christian?" when the better question is, "Who should I be?" Keep in mind that people (yourself included) can't behave as mature Christians (Level 3) until they have matured as Christians (Levels 1 and 2).

Level 3: Walk. Level 3 discipleship involves supporting people in their daily walks (see Colossians 2:6).

- What characterizes the spiritually mature person in each of the following areas?

Spiritual life

_____
_____
_____
_____

Mind

_____
_____
_____
_____

Emotions

_____
_____
_____
_____

Will

_____

_____

_____

_____

Relationships

_____

_____

_____

_____

- Think about your home, your school, your youth group and society in general. Where in these areas do you need help functioning more like a believer? To whom can you go for discipling and prayer support?

Immature believers don't need to constantly be told what they should do. Instead, let's celebrate with them what Christ has already done and help them become who they already are in Him. Amen? Amen!

CONCEPTS FOR COUNSELING

If you have a compassionate heart and a knowledge and love of the Lord, God can use you to encourage and instruct young people with problems. The goal of such counseling is to help people experience freedom in Christ so that they can move on to maturity and fruitfulness in their walks with Him. Here are five practical tips.

1. *Help People Identify Root Issues.* Psalm 1:1-3 compares the mature Christian to a fruitful tree. The fruitfulness of the branches above the ground is the result of the fertility of the soil and the health of the root system that spreads into it.

   - How can this image help you if someone comes to you for counseling? What does this image encourage you to address?

   - What are some of the emotions and situations that can prompt someone to seek Christian counseling?

- For each item you listed above, what is a possible root cause for the primary emotions touched by the situation (rejection, fear, unforgiveness, false belief system, rebellion)?

- What has this discussion of root issues helped you understand about yourself?

2. *Encourage Emotional Honesty.* People are generally willing to share what has happened to them, but they are not usually willing to share their failures or how they feel about them.

   - With whom do you have an easy time being emotionally honest? Why?

   - What can you do to encourage a person you're counseling to be emotionally honest? (Consider your body language, your verbal responses, the setting of the conversation, and so forth.)

3. *Share the Truth.* When Christians seek advice or counsel, it's usually because their problems have caused them to think there is something wrong with them. They may feel that God can't possibly love them.

   - When have you had such feelings? How did you deal with them? Be specific.

   - Based on your own experience and what you've learned in *Stomping Out the Darkness*, what will you do for someone who comes to you feeling something's wrong with her and God can't love her?

4. *Call for a Response.* Your role in advising and counseling your friends is to share the truth in love and pray that the person will choose to accept it.

   - Why is prayer key to any counseling situation? Give two or three reasons.

   - Why is the fact that you cannot choose change for your friend (only your friend can do that!) freeing news to you as the counselor?

5. *Help Them Plan for the Future.* Sometimes when we're in the depths of despair, the future can look pretty bleak.

  • What truth can you offer someone feeling overwhelmed by problems and despair?

  • What practical steps can you encourage that person to take? More specifically, what kinds of supportive relationships will you propose?

  • What will you teach about the difference between goals and desires (see chapter 7)?

You and I are what we are by the grace of God. All we have and can hope for—as disciplers and disciples, as counselors and people in need of counsel—is based on who we are in Christ. May your life and your ministry therefore be shaped by your devotion to Him and the conviction that He is the way, the truth and the life.

START STOMPING!

Try It, You'll Like It! God calls us as individuals to follow Him, but He wants us to do so in a community. So if you're not plugged into a Christian community, make it your goal to find a youth group within the next few weeks. You need the group—and the group needs you. If you're already involved in a youth group, take a step toward greater involvement. That can mean anything from behind-the-scenes service to the group to an up-front leadership role. God has just the place for you!

Your Tree of Life. Look again at the diagram on page 143 of the text. The top tree reflects a barren life; the bottom, a fruitful life. Now draw your own tree. What root problem(s) are you dealing with? What food does your root system need? What instruction would you benefit from? In what areas of your life (spiritual life, mind, emotions, will, relationships) do you need encouragement and challenge (i.e., discipling)? Where do you need to do some pruning? Having answered these questions, develop a plan for taking care of your tree. Consider whom you can ask for help with the gardening. In other words, who would you like to disciple you? Also figure out where you will go to get the nurturing (true belief system, acceptance, forgiveness, freedom, submission) that you need to bear fruit. Keep in mind, too, that prayer is like oxygen for your tree of life.

A Prayer for All of Us. Whether you're in need of Christian support and counsel right now or it's your turn to offer that kind of support and guidance, this prayer is for you: "God, grant me the serenity to accept the things I cannot change, the courage to change the things I can, and the wisdom to know the difference." Put these words to music, write them on a poster, etch them onto a piece of metal or burn them into wood, draw a picture representing serenity, courage and wisdom—whatever you do, make this prayer a part of your life.

> *God, thank You that I can live out my faith as a part of a team. There are times when I realize I just can't do it alone—and I realize I never would have come to know You without Your people reaching out to me with Your love. Thanks for all the folks You've placed in my life to help me learn more about You and help me become more like Your Son. And thank You for the privilege of being able to help others who are at a different place in their Christian walks. Whether it's my turn to disciple or be discipled, to offer counsel or receive it, may I do so in the solid knowledge of Your love, Your light and Your truth. Thank You that I am Your child—and thank You for sending Your Son to make that possible. It is in His name I pray. Amen.*

STRENGTH GIVERS

These words are *for* you and *about* you! As you read each day's verse, ask yourself, "How would my life be different if I could live out this truth?"—and ask God to help you do so.

Monday:	John 15:15
Tuesday:	Ephesians 2:19
Wednesday:	1 Corinthians 15:10
Thursday:	2 Corinthians 5:18-19
Friday:	Galatians 3:26; 4:6

Books and Resources by
Dr. Neil T. Anderson

Victory Over the Darkness
(Regal Books, 2000)

The Bondage Breaker
(Harvest House Publishers, 2000)

Beta: The Next Step in Your Journey with Christ
(Regal Books, 2004)

Free
(with Dave Park, Regal Books, 2005)

For ministry information, visit
www.discipleshipcounselingministries.org
www.hispassionministries.org

Contact Freedom in Christ Ministries at the following:
Freedom in Christ Ministries
9051 Executive Park Drive, Suite 503
Knoxville, TN 37923
E-mail: info@ficm.org / Website: www.ficm.org

For product, contact:
E-3 Resources
317 Main Street, Suite 207
Franklin, Tennessee 327064
(888) 354-9411
info@e3resources.org